The
Stupendous
Story of
Us

T0083597

For Jennie, who kept me believing

Published in 2022 by
Unify, an imprint of Unicorn Publishing Group LLP
5 Newburgh Street
London
W1F 7RG
www.unicornpublishing.org

ISBN 978 1 914414 54 1
10 9 8 7 6 5 4 3 2 1

Design by newtonworks.uk
Printed by Short Run Press, Exeter, UK

Also available on Amazon by the same author
in the series
Empires of the Mind

We Are More Than Our Brains
Putting our minds to neuroscience
No Man is an Island
How pain, suffering and hope bind us to each other
The Mosaic of the Mind
Where does our mind go in sleep, dreams, hypnosis and meditation?
In Our Right Mind
Sex, drug, kicks and control
Mountains of the Mind
How we get depth from flatness
The Mirror of the Mind
Seeing personally, seeing really and seeing sanely
The Smart Mind   *For more information* https://www.trevorrollings.com
A natural history of intelligence   *Join the conversation* trevor@trevorrollings.com

FROM **BIG BANG** TO **BIG BROTHER**
IN FIFTEEN FRANTIC CHAPTERS

The
Stupendous
Story of
Us

TREVOR ROLLINGS

UNIFY

Terracotta Warrior
His body is made of fired earth, but his mind is free to ponder his Stupendous Story.
A penny for his thoughts?

Only connect.   *E M Forster*

It turns out that humanity's problem is not knowing how we came to be or even how the universe came up with us, but how we are, how we behave, and what, if anything, we can do about it.   *Richard Holloway*

Contents

On the Nature of Things

Where do we come from? What are we? Where are we going? *Paul Gauguin*

These three questions form the title of a canvas painted by Paul Gauguin in Tahiti in 1897. Life for the figures in the frame seems innocent enough, but their island idyll, if such it had ever been, had already been corrupted by greed and disease following the arrival of paradise-seekers like himself.

No wonder then that his questions sound like Sphinx-like riddles, with answers that are at best elliptical: we come from our mothers, and we are heading for the grave. As regards what happens in between, all is mystery in the midst of a life that is at best uncertain.

But we keep asking, because it is in our nature to desire to know. It is not long before we realise that reality is a jigsaw, only one corner of it illuminated by science. To add to its complexity we are given no picture on the lid at the outset.

What's it all about?

We can ask this question of scientists, philosophers, even our best friends, but ultimately we have to find the answer within ourselves.

About six hundred years ago, after fifteen hundred years of Christianity, Europe was beginning to pose Gauguin's questions afresh, without recourse to the Bible. New ideas were abroad. A savvy manuscript-hunter had found an ancient text mouldering in the crypt of a German monastery. It was an extended Latin poem by Lucretius, called 'On the Nature of Things'. Written just before the birth of Christ, it had been copied often enough to survive the ravages of time.

Lucretius anticipated the spirit of Gauguin's questions perfectly by appealing to reason, not revelation. If Nature is our guide, there is no room for gods. But he also realised that the world of Things is to a large extent the creation of our mind, writing 'You alone govern the nature of things. Without you nothing emerges into the light of day, without you nothing is joyous or lovely'.

Modern science has largely vindicated Lucretius's answers to Gauguin's 'how' questions: there is movement without a mover, and design without a designer. Answers to his 'why' questions about the point of it all have remained much more elusive. There is no theory of everything, only intertwining thoughts and feelings that we must weave into a unified understanding.

We now know things about the natural world that Lucretius could only guess at, but there is much we still don't know and perhaps never will. Meanwhile, our understanding of our inner world remains an enigma. Nothing is obvious, and much is contested.

Even so, this book tries to give Gauguin some answers. The story it tells is stupendous because it is full of surprises and defies the odds. Its pace is frantic because learning is long and life is short. Ideas, seen together and clearly stated, can help to orient our mind towards a sustainable future. We may never arrive, but the joy is in the journeying and the effort repays itself. Knowledge is power, and we have a right to know.

Seeing ourselves through the lens of deep time might throw new light on some of today's intractable problems, and our own contradictions. If we see our story as an integrated narrative, we can begin to understand our role as actors in its drama. We see only fragments, but everything is connected, and if we are to move the world, we need a place to stand.

Each chapter is designed to be read comfortably in one sitting, linked to the others but telling its own tale. Like any story, there is a progression of ideas, but there's no reason not to start at the end and work backwards.

1 How did our story begin?

The Big Bang, the beginning of time, multiple worlds, the birth of planet Earth, energy and entropy, the emergence of life, chance and necessity, evolution, the death of the dinosaurs, the rise of the mammals.

It is not how things are in the world that is mystical, but that it exists. *Ludwig Wittgenstein*

> *Science allows us to peer into the mystery of Deep Time, but it cannot give us an ultimate explanation for our being here.*

Alpha to Omega

The stories we tell each other always begin in fixed points of time and space, and this includes our account of the origin of the universe. Scientists inform us that time and space began with a specific event of cosmic significance called the Big Bang.

This is however a very recent idea. At the dawning of human thought, philosophers assumed the notions of eternity and infinity. The universe has always existed as an idea in the Divine Mind. God came before physics, and the solid stuff we see around us is but an imperfect copy of a greater perfect whole. For the mediaeval poet Dante, it is love that moves the sun and stars, not gravity.

Over the last four hundred years scientists have made remarkable challenges to this poetic view of our beginnings. Gone is the idea of a Grand Firmament towering over our brief lives while we pass through Purgatory. Now we have an evolving universe expanding into curved space-time, more like a self-generating superbrain than the bedtime story of a benign Creator.

Scientists have slowly pieced together *how* the universe began by natural means, leaving the supernatural *why* of creation to theologians. There is a world, it is knowable, and it is in constant motion, with no need of a Prime Mover. Any meanings, motives and purposes, human or divine, are put there by us. If, like astrologers, we long to see love written across the heavens, it will shine back to us. If, like astronomers, we listen out for the echo of a star collapsing into a black hole, we will hear it.

Physicists give us not the Book of Genesis but the Standard Model. It can't yet account for the blinding flash that set the universe going, but it holds firm for everything that came after. Whether we insist that God is a necessary hypothesis to explain a one-off Act of Creation, or look to classical physics to describe the ceaseless maelstrom of forces and particles that holds us in place, there was an event nearly fourteen billion years ago nicknamed the Big Bang.

No-one was there to witness the birth of the universe, but the Big Bang is to date our best possible explanation, based on the principle of sufficient reason. We know there was an almighty explosion, because we can measure the cosmic background radiation from that time and use the red shift effect to date the age of constellations as they formed.

Some balk at the idea of being humanly stranded amidst such vastness and indifference. They insist that there is an Uncaused Causer behind our being here, and providence in the fall of a sparrow. The universe is the creation of an all-powerful perfectly good Being. Others feel no need to strive after supernatural causes or reasons. They accept our being here as a brute fact, and that's that.

Either way, once set in motion, the universe became a mathematical probability, with no need for a remote deity outside of time and space, or the sustaining love of a personal God. The Big Bang triggered a race that began in heat and violence and ended in microbes and Mozart. Out of a blind universe arose a sighted human mind.

However we try to strip the veil from the face of God, or put nature to the sword of scientific investigation, something came from nothing, a paradoxical effect without a cause. This makes no sense to our feeble intellect unless we grasp that 'nothing' wasn't empty in the first place. It was an energy field waiting to inflate into matter through a quantum fluctuation, not just once, but potentially into eternity. Every solid thing we see around us is frozen energy, held in place long enough to serve as the building blocks of the universe.

Ninety per cent of what is 'out there' is dark matter, the glue that holds the galaxies together. So far our instruments have not detected it, so we cannot yet claim to know the Mind of God. Or perhaps we are just asking the wrong questions. Physicists welcome the notion of their models being found wanting, because that takes them ever closer to what could be right.

The crucible of creation

Within three hundred million years of the Big Bang, there arose the Cosmic Dawn. After aeons of blackness, the first stars started to coalesce as giant furnaces, not just forging the elements in our body but also providing heat and light. If Genesis got one thing right, it was God's first command 'Let there be light', because without light, there is no life.

Matter is still being created in the cosmic crucible, galaxies ceaselessly rushing away from us in a universe expanding like a giant balloon. There are billions of solar systems, and here we sit in one of them on a tiny planet called Earth, seven billion of us scarily alone in the eternal silence of the infinite spaces.

We survive, according to the Anthropic Principle, because we inhabit a Goldilocks zone where the forces seem to be fine-tuned, strong enough to prevent our soft bodies from flying apart and weak enough not to crush them. This suggests to some that the universe knew we were coming: we are just the right size, made of just the right stuff, inhabiting the best of all possible worlds, destined to be the pinnacle of evolution.

Others are not so sure. We are made of raw chemicals smelted in the fires of ancient stars, suggesting that our mere existence is a chance outcome of literally astronomical proportions. The universe had to be this old, vast and empty to have the time to prepare the ingredients for 'cooking' a mind like ours, capable of thinking these thoughts. The fact that the universe seems intelligible to our mind, satisfying as that is, is an accident of nature, not proof of divine ancestry.

Random as our being here seems, it is no more than a mathematical probability, which means we are unlikely to be unique or alone. There are so many billions of galaxies that one of them was bound to be just right for us, because computationally, anything that can happen does happen somewhere. There *must* be stars supporting life on other planets like ours, even if working to slightly different laws.

This leads to the possibility of multiple worlds. Somewhere out there, on a planet in a galaxy far, far away, there might be someone like us, thinking our thoughts. Even weirder, if we follow the speculations of string theorists, there may be as many as eleven dimensions, and ways of travelling between them through wormholes in time. There could be parallel worlds millimetres away from us, but we can't see or step into them.

If the universe has no boundary, there is no point trying to travel to its edge, nor is there a centre to start from. Einstein taught us that matter causes space-time to curve, perhaps into the shape of a doughnut turned inside out. If we do blast off, we might meet ourselves coming back.

After such a dramatic beginning, how might our story end, with yet another mighty bang, or just a pathetic whimper? As the stars slowly burn out, the clock might go into reverse, returning us to a vast, dark, freezing expanse of nothing. After being born in fire, we will end in ice. Alternatively, human activity, having pumped so much carbon into the atmosphere, will switch our climate to irreversible defrost, and we will all drown.

There is a further possibility, but it won't help us any time soon in our relentless passage from Alpha to Omega. Time might be warped. We could be in the middle of an inexhaustible sequence of cosmic bounces between Big Bangs and Big Crunches, a cyclical karma of particles creating and destroying each other into eternity.

The appearance of life

Planet Earth, which started to form out of clouds of swirling gas four and a half billion years ago, still has a long way to run. Its surface was initially molten rock and its atmosphere was toxic, but within half a billion years, it was cool enough for the first microbes to appear on the scene, largely carbon-based, because carbon is both abundant and capable of bonding with other atoms to form the complex molecular chains necessary to generate and sustain life.

Energy flows and heat gradients provide a clue as to how life on earth might have been given a free ride. The sun is hotter than the Earth, and plants learned early on to harness its surplus through photosynthesis. Gradually their green alchemy helped them not just to convert sunlight to energy, but also to expel oxygen, thereby creating the troposphere, the thin film of breathable air around the earth on which all life depends. Life could now feed on life, fuelling itself through complex food chains. The mighty elephant could grow strong by eating vast quantities of grass and leaves.

But grass and elephants were a long way down the track. The first life forms were neither plant nor animal, though they had already mastered one trick necessary for the evolution of life: they could exchange chemicals with their surroundings, carefully controlling what comes in and what goes out.

These organisms, capable of functioning as individual living entities, might have come into being many times, perhaps fermenting in boiling vents under the ocean, sparking after a lightning bolt, even arriving from outer space. Many became extinct before they got started, but it needed only one to become the mother of all life on earth.

For this to happen, there had to be several 'phase transitions' in the evolution of life. The first came two billion years ago, when one bacterium developed the ability to live inside another. Enter the nucleated cell, information-hungry and with enough orchestrated chemical wizardry to turn a caterpillar into a butterfly.

By one billion years ago, these super-cells were starting to engage in sexual reproduction, which is the driver of evolution. Life's urge is to create order, which death in the form of entropy is constantly trying to destroy. Life's defence against this is to combine DNA through genes. In this way, information is not lost but transformed into a new organism that can temporarily maintain its boundaries against the encroaching world and stave off dissolution, for a generation at least, which is the nearest any of us will ever get to immortality.

This sets the stage for multi-celled organisms such as plants and animals, in which embryonic stem cells could specialise as stalk, leaf, petal, heart, liver or brain cells. Life could now diversify into the various kingdoms that colonise the branches on Darwin's Tree of Life, but there are many blurred boundaries. A Venus flytrap looks like a plant, but it 'catches' its prey by closing the jaws of its sticky leaves, able to 'count' up to three before it strikes.

This clever ploy is not sufficient to make it an animal, which requires a motivating 'anima', or the power of locomotion. Flytraps stay in one place, but animals have to move about for a living. This calls for a brain at the 'business' end of the organism, and a nervous system to coordinate the movement of its limbs. Even humble earthworms have to do a lot of moving and thinking if they are to stay alive. As proof that our human ancestry is shared with all other life forms on the planet, we share seventy per cent of our genes with them.

By five hundred million years ago, which is a blink in the evolutionary eye, things start to move relatively quickly. As evolution rolled the dice more and more in every possible design-space, ceaselessly experimenting, it was able to select the gossamer of a bird's wing one day and the grossness of a shark's teeth the next.

Fish with backbones morphed into vertebrates colonising the land, equipped with lungs to breathe air. They were accompanied by seed-bearing plants, winged insects, amphibians, reptiles and, as every child knows, terrifying creatures called dinosaurs, large and small, some with skeletons light enough to perfect the art of flight.

Whether we believe that evolution by natural selection alone is capable of generating such 'endless forms most beautiful and most wonderful', as Darwin put it, there is a limit. In our imagination angels, fairies and unicorns possess wings, but they could never evolve in nature. To lift themselves aloft, they would need chest muscles the size of their body.

Other myths have also quietly disappeared. For centuries vitalism ruled the roost: there is a spirit that breathes life into inert matter and disappears with death. This quaint belief might be in abeyance, but we still talk of a life 'force', we are drawn instinctively to people who possess 'vitality', and we're not likely to start a conversation with a mannequin in a shop window.

Another vanished belief is the spontaneous generation of life. We no longer believe that swallows mysteriously emerge from muddy pools in the spring, or that mice are spawned in piles of dirty washing. Life proceeds only from life, which takes us all the way back to a single common ancestor simmering gently in what Darwin described as a 'warm little pond'.

Understanding evolution

If Isaac Newton explained to us why apples fall on our head, it was Charles Darwin who transformed our understanding of evolution. It is not designed by God, but driven by biology, not planned but possessed of an iron logic, which can look like a kind of purpose. There is disagreement whether it crawls or jumps, but it explains the seemingly pointless, such as why males possess nipples.

Every niche offers survival opportunities and organisms that make the most of them survive to breed, out-competing those that don't. The fox struggles in the hedgehog's world and vice versa. Cunning works for one as a survival strategy, and a prickly coat for the other.

'Survival of the fittest' was applied to Darwin's ideas about evolution, but it is not a phrase Darwin ever used, because it is misleading. It's not about superiority, or winning and losing, but adaptability. We don't carry any genes from ancestors who failed to fight off disease, stay out of fights, self-repair and find a mate to raise a family.

Charles Darwin
1809–1882

Darwin's ideas about evolution were 'in the air' before he published them in 1859, but they still caused quite a stir. Some reject them even today, but not only have they stood the test for a hundred and fifty years, they are confirmed by every new finding.

Planet Earth might still be ruled by dinosaurs, which were doing very well as a genus, had not chance entered the fray. Chance cannot be controlled, only tamed in accordance with a new necessity. About sixty-five million years ago, a meteor struck the Earth. The resulting cloud of dust that enveloped the planet didn't directly kill all the dinosaurs, but it blocked the sunlight, stunting the growth of the plants they grazed on and starving the prey they hunted.

Out of disaster comes opportunity. Up to this point mammals had featured very little in Earth's story, but the fossil record shows that certain small shrew-like mammals were able to survive the long winter that killed the dinosaurs. This was their moment, and they grasped it, not consciously but by endless mutations and slices of good fortune which gradually made them bigger, stronger, faster and smarter.

By now the Earth's climate and atmosphere were just right for all the animals that were loaded onto Noah's Ark. From our perspective, chief among them was the primate family. We often hear that we share ninety-eight per cent of our genome with chimpanzees and bonobos. They show great cleverness in the wild, and in captivity they exhibit skill in understanding what we previously considered to be unique human features, such as symbol-recognition and ability to use sign language.

We are not however 'descended' from chimps or bonobos in any meaningful sense, or from any other type of ape. We broke away from them eight million years ago, allowing tens of thousands of generations for human intelligence and consciousness to evolve. For better or worse, we are now the dominant organism on the planet.

From Big Bang to Big Brother

bya, mya and kya = billions, millions or thousands of years ago

13.8	bya	The **Big Bang**
13.5	bya	**Cosmic Dawn:** first stars formed
4.5	bya	**Earth** formed
4	bya	Single-celled **prokaryotes** appear in the oceans
3	bya	First oxygen-based **bacteria**
2	bya	First **eukaryotes** or nucleated cells
1.2	bya	First **sexual reproduction**
600	mya	First **multi-celled organisms**
500	mya	First **fungi**
450	mya	**Fish** with backbones evolve in the oceans
410	mya	First **seed-bearing** plants on land
400	mya	First **cycads** and winged **insects**
350	mya	Dry land colonised by **amphibians**
300	mya	First **reptiles** and **conifers**
240	mya	Dominance of **dinosaurs**
210	mya	First **birds**
200	mya	First small **mammals**
210	mya	First flowering **plants**
65	mya	**Dinosaurs wiped out**
40	mya	**Primates** evolve
8	mya	**Hominins**, our human ancestors, split from chimps
4.5	mya	Fully **upright posture**
3.5	mya	Laetoli footprints and '**Lucy**' skeleton found
2.5	mya	**Tool-making** appears
1.5	mya	**Brain size** doubles
1	mya	**Homo erectus** in East Africa
850	kya	Erectus **migrates** into Asia and Europe, with no survivors
100	kya	First true humans, **Homo sapiens**
50	kya	Sapiens reaches **Middle East, Australia, Europe**
40	kya	**Neanderthals** die out
35	kya	Sapiens reaches **Americas**
	1949	George Orwell writes '1984' featuring '**Big Brother**'

2 Why us?

Walking upright, brain boost, fire, tool-making, cognitive revolution, cave art, shamanism, hunting, consciousness, migration out of Africa, savagery and civilisation.

They, hand in hand, with wandering steps and slow,
Through Eden took their solitary way.   *John Milton*

> *As part of the animal kingdom, we understand ourselves best in the light of evolution.*

Journey out of Eden

Every story needs its heroes to drive its plot forward, so picture the scene: a mother and child are walking across soft sand, holding hands. All they leave behind is footprints. Touching but not unusual, we might think, until we realise that this happened three and a half million years ago. The footprints, not discovered until 1978, were preserved forever by a freak of time and nature at Laetoli in Tanzania, the Eden in East Africa where our ancestors evolved.

It's not just the antiquity of the prints that is remarkable. It's the fact that these hominin forebears were *walking*. This little family were Australopithecines, or southern apes, characterised by an upright posture. Slowly, as they made their faltering way, they were taking giant steps to becoming Homo sapiens.

We even have a body to go with the footprints. The skeleton of 'Lucy', dating from around the same time as the footprints and named after the Beatles' song 'Lucy in the Sky with Diamonds', had been found in nearby Ethiopia four years earlier. She is only a metre tall but she is distinctly a proto-human. Her face is ape-like, but her erect gait carries her towards a human future.

Scientists are slowly piecing together our evolutionary back-story. We all bear, as Darwin reminded us, the 'indelible stamp of our lowly origins', because there was no sudden arrival at modern humans. Adam and Eve were not created anew but were born with navels, umbilically attached to as many as twenty species of the human sub-family that preceded them, though not all alive at the same time. New species are still being identified from shards of bone and skull. Homo Erectus lasted two million years, making tools, using fire, hunting with spears and enjoying a degree of self-awareness.

Our last fellow hominins to die out were the Neanderthals about forty thousand years ago. They left behind some tools, rock art and hints that they placed gifts in the graves of their dead, strong evidence of technical ability, culture and a degree of empathy.

For a while there was speculation that we drove them to extinction, but their demise might owe more to a combination of limited diet, cooling climate, less developed use of fire, and disease. Their brain capacity was bigger than ours, but when it comes to smartness, size isn't everything. It's not about how many neurons there are but how they are differentiated and organised. Our slightly smaller brains were more tightly connected with newly evolved 'thinking' networks, giving us the edge in adapting to setbacks.

Neanderthal populations were sparse and resources scarce, but we share about four per cent of their DNA, as well as some Denisovan genes, another type of Homo that disappeared around the same time, so there must have been contact, friendly or otherwise.

The disappearance of all of our Homo cousins means that chimpanzees and bonobos are now our nearest 'relatives', but we are not descended from them, nor is there a 'missing link' between us and them. We parted company from them eight million years ago and have evolved along very different lines.

Standing on our own two feet

Alone among the primate family, when it comes to getting around, we are most comfortable standing up, not crawling on all fours. We occasionally see chimpanzees stand upright in the trees of their forest home but that is not their preferred posture on the ground.

It wasn't a case of our ancestors 'choosing' to leave the trees and stand erect. As the climate dried, the trees left them. The lonely and dangerous expanses of the African savannah became our landscape of evolutionary adaptation, the factory setting for our physique and psychology, even though most of us now live cosseted lives in crowded cities.

Foraging and hunting game on open grassland proved to be much easier on two legs, though we can't simply attribute human status to walking upright. The fossil record suggests that other now extinct species of ape might have beaten us to it.

In our case change of posture and locomotion triggered a domino effect, starting with substantial modification of our primate skeleton. Walking upright frees the hands for much wider use, opening the door to tool-making. It remodels the shape of the spine and lifts up the eyes, making us predominantly visual creatures, stimulating the growth of our massive visual cortex, which takes up a quarter of our brain space.

It leads to the shedding of fur to enable our sweat glands to keep us cool. This means we can become efficient long-distance joggers, carrying water in gourds so that we can run down an antelope until it collapses of exhaustion. The boost of protein found in meat and the social cooperation required to organise a successful hunt further fuel an expansion in brain size, giving us the largest brain in proportion to our body size of any creature on the planet.

By one and a half million years ago brain size has doubled, giving us our domed skulls and egg-head appearance. Our sapiens brain is now so big that mothers struggle to give birth to their babies, whose brains continue to expand for another nine months after birth. In that sense, we are all born nine months premature.

Fixing the precise moment we became truly human is like trying to pin down where adolescence begins and ends, but people we would recognise as fellow humans began to appear around a hundred thousand years ago. Not only has the configuration of our brain hardly changed since, it has also shrunk slightly from its prehistoric peak.

We will never be able to reconstruct the twisting path of cause and effect to full Homo status, and new finds keep pushing dates further back. No single factor marks us as unique. Bones leave physical traces, but what mattered in our evolution is what we can't see. As well as a big brain on top of an upright body we needed the conscious awareness of a moral, believing animal.

This emerged slowly from our willingness to share and cooperate, grounded in mutual trust. Such emotional maturity calls for empathy, which began in our mother's arms. As she grew increasingly hairless around three million years ago, we could no longer cling to her back. She had to pick us up to carry us long distances, allowing us to gaze into her eyes, tightening our bond of attachment to her. Our eyes developed white sclera, enabling us to read each other's mind through detecting direction of gaze. The main attraction of face to face love-making is the intimate entwining of the eyes.

Without this emotional connectedness, families would have failed to flourish, alliances beyond immediate kin could not been made, and cultural ideas would have died with their creators. The reason chimpanzees don't rule the world is that they spend more time fighting and squabbling than building a better society.

Fire and tools

Other aspects of our evolutionary success are more obvious. The myth of Prometheus stealing fire from the gods is based on real breakthroughs and benefits in deep time. Fire wards off predators, enabling not only precious babies to survive but also more grandparents, who provide useful help and teach vital skills. It creates a camp fire culture around which knowledge can be shared and stories passed on.

Cooking detoxifies food and makes it more digestible, requiring a smaller gut, which frees up more energy for calorie-hungry brain-building. Tough uncooked food requires powerful jaw muscles that clamp the cranium, but softer cooked food allows the skull to be remodelled. An enlarged mouth cavity allows the tongue to move more freely, and a lowered larynx frees the vocal cords to produce a wider range of sounds, paving the way for spoken language, a 'trick' that other apes cannot perform.

We cannot say that tools or language 'caused' the big brain or made us human. Many animals use tools and communicate in sophisticated ways, and Homo erectus was quietly fashioning tools and chatting away for a million years before brain size doubled.

When the cognitive revolution finally arrived about a hundred thousand years ago, it marked a giant leap in the human story. It was caused not by a handful of genes but by powerful brain circuits, each evolved separately, but combining to form an integrated collective that defines the human mind: organising the world systematically, thinking symbolically, reading the thoughts of others, and manipulating the environment.

Together these cognitive programs created a new way of experiencing reality, which we call consciousness. They also generated a lever to change the world, which we call technology, and a storehouse of wisdom, which we call culture.

Toolmaking not only extended the power of the body; it also transformed our mental capacity. In order to make a tool we have to think sequentially and precisely, increasing communication between both sides of our brain. Toolmaking also sharpens our attention and perceptual range. When we use a knife, we focus on the point of its blade, not on our hand. When we use a computer, our mind travels far beyond the confines of our skull.

Tools were engineers of change, enhancing control over nature. Rocks could crush bones to release their nourishing marrow, blades could skin animals, axes could fell trees to build shelters. Making tools was a highly social activity, facilitating the exchange of ideas and the passing on of skills to the young.

Toolmaking also fired the imagination because the use and effects of a tool have to be envisioned before the flint is struck. One thing has to be seen in terms of another, which calls for symbolic thinking. The inventor has to 'see' that it is much more deadly to attach an arrowhead to a spear, or fire a smaller version of it from a bow, as well as being much safer for the hunter.

Cave art

Large dangerous animals were always a threat, so it is unsurprising that our ancestors sought out safer ways of killing them from a distance, and rock shelters for protection. We know these things because of the dramatic paintings of animals that have been found deep inside caves in central Europe, dating from around thirty thousand years ago. Some are much earlier, in which case they must have been painted by Neanderthals.

The Sorcerer

This enigmatic drawing, dating from 13,000 BCE, was discovered in 1914 in a cave in France. It has been nicknamed The Sorcerer, but we can only guess the ritual purpose of a shaman dressing up in an animal skin.

The cave art tells of a hunter-gatherer past. Chimps are poor at throwing, but Lucy's skeleton shows that she was capable of launching a projectile straight and hard. Twenty humans, coordinating their efforts and aiming their missiles carefully, could surround and bring down even the largest predator.

But hunter-gathering was no Edenic idyll. Prey was hard to find and even harder to catch. It is likely that the women folk provided more calories for the growing clan by gathering roots and fruits than the macho men managed to bring down with their makeshift weapons.

Hunting did however provide essential protein, as well as lay the foundations for community and cooperation. The lone hunter bringing a kill back to the camp was under an obligation to share the meat with others, especially if the animal was the totem of the clan. Powerful taboos prevented him from keeping certain parts of the carcase for himself.

Cave art captures some of the ritual surrounding hunting, most notably the ineffable mystery of death as necessary to sustain life. Killing animals so that humans might live creates cognitive dissonance, partly resolved by worshipping the creature to be slain, as a way of atoning for slaughtering it.

Such sentiments gave rise to the shaman as mediator between this world and the next, in what might have been the first hint of a religious sensibility. Donning the hide of the beast to perform a fertility dance established a degree of control over the animal world and united the clan against external enemies. His magic might even have extended to human birth, our ancestors not grasping the link between sex and reproduction until as recently as ten thousand years ago.

The enigma of consciousness

The evolution of consciousness is the hardest to explain. Lucy lived a short and precarious life, but as her brain became populated by more and more thinking modules she needed a way of centralising the operation, an inner model of who she was, and a master of ceremonies to manage her feelings. Her mind was a noisy theatre of possibilities which had to be distilled into the voice of a single actor.

This 'director' is hard to locate in the brain. We can have half our brain surgically removed for medical reasons, and still wake up fully conscious. Even more puzzlingly, the octopus's consciousness is spread throughout its eight tentacles.

Our peculiar sense of *what it feels like to be me* can't be reduced to the eighty-five billion neurons going about their business like mini-bots. Somewhere, somehow, in ways neuroscientists still cannot explain, chemistry and information are conjured into awareness of our own existence, to a degree that we do not think possible in a stone, tree or robot.

Consciousness is not just a matter of *thinking*, which evolved relatively late in the day. Life for our ancestors was primarily about *feeling*, which emanates from the much older brain stem that we share with all other animals. Are my friends plotting against me? Can I trust this stranger approaching me? Have I offended the gods in some way?

Our brain does not develop the circuitry to articulate thoughts of this complexity until our third or fourth year, which is why we need so much post-natal care. Then, when it comes fully on stream, *knowing that we know* can drive us to distraction. In that sense, consciousness can be a curse, the consequence of biting into the forbidden apple, its taste sweet at first, then tinged with the bitterness of knowing that we are venal, and must surely die.

Consciousness feels so real because it evolved to confront us with *things that matter* while we are awake. Our senses are so busy filling our head with inputs that we can't pay attention to all of them all of the time. We need a mechanism for shining the spotlight on the one thing we ought to be paying attention to right now. This is me having these thoughts, and that rustle in the bushes might be a lion creeping up on me.

But we can't live our whole life in high-intensity close-up. We also need our consciousness to work as a lantern, spreading a wider light. Who else is with me, why are we making this journey together in the first place, and where do we think we are heading? We are back to Gauguin's three questions.

Consciousness is spread throughout nature. We hardly balk at stepping on an ant, but we persuade ourselves that our pet dog has a mind. Even if it can't *think* like us, we know it can *feel* the way we do, which is why we don't leave it locked in a hot car all day.

And yet we readily factory-farm and eat pigs which are just as intelligent as dogs, and have the same nervous system as us. Perhaps future generations will look back in horror on our abuse of animals and addiction to fossil fuels, as we do on history's slave owners or present day people traffickers.

It seems reasonable to presume however that no other animal reflects on its being here in the way we do. We might therefore justifiably claim that, if the universe is conscious in any sense, it is in and through us. We are the only species capable of feeling regret that the universe might end tomorrow.

Civilisation

Eight hundred and fifty thousand years ago, powered by their curiosity and bur-
geoning consciousness, small groups of Homo erectus staged the first migrations
out of their African cradle of mankind, south to the Cape, north to Europe and
east to Asia, as far eventually as Australia and into the Americas, pushing into new
territory at an average rate of two miles a year.

None of them survived, though new finds are regularly made outside Africa of
pre-human cultures that, given different slightly different circumstances, might
have flourished to people the earth. As it is, it seems that a major push Out of
Africa around sixty thousand years ago by sapiens forebears was the progenitor of
all the languages, beliefs and cultures of today's global population. Modern Euro-
peans are likely to be carrying African hunter-gatherer, Middle Eastern agricul-
turalist and Eurasian pastoralist DNA in equal measure, making nonsense of any
notions of single origin, genetic purity or racial supremacy.

Nor was there a steady trajectory to what we might regard as civilisation. Some
groups farmed for a while then reverted to hunter-gathering, perhaps on a sea-
sonal cycle. Other groups had flat political structures, or were led by chieftains
who were not dynastic potentates but charismatic leaders chosen for their ability
to guide the clan through hard times.

Just over five thousand years ago, through accidents of history and geography,
some groups became civilised before others, as in enjoying the benefits of living
in an organised community. City-dwelling created the conditions for population
growth. Nomads have to carry their children with them, so produce offspring on
a four-year cycle. City-dwellers, with predictable food supplies, could reproduce
every second year.

This boost in population created a surplus of time and resources, allowing
enterprise, art and science to flourish. Ideas circulate slowly among hunter gatherers, but cities, with their extra security and cooperation, encouraged diversity of
thinking and sped up technological progress.

'Civilisation' as a cultural ideal is something of a mixed bag morally. The
Romans could enjoy the benefits of running water in the public baths in the
morning, then enjoy the bloodshed of gladiatorial entertainment in the afternoon.
Both habits were regarded as high achievements of their imperial superiority, but
civilisation has flourished best when there has been open exchange of material
goods and intellectual property. The first cities built walls for protection from

marauding barbarians, but those that built trading networks prospered to become innovation hubs and racial melting pots.

All civilisations have their golden age but they occur at different times, creating an imbalance of power. By the seventeenth century the West had the technology and appetite to conquer, colonise and grab the resources of civilisations that had lapsed into decadence, or regions of the world that were less developed. Non-Europeans were seen at best as noble savages, at worst as primitive natives who were incapable of rational thought, unable to feel pain and lacking a soul. They could therefore be denied their rights, driven off their land and enslaved.

We now know that beneath the skin we all share the same default blood supply to our body and brain. We all belong to a form of civilisation that is uniquely human, based on the taming of nature and sharing of ideas. We are all Lucy's children, big-brained, intelligent, self-aware and capable of every human emotion. Of all the gifts of consciousness, this is the truth of which we need to be most mindful.

Cognitive and Cultural Revolutions

2	mya	Crude cutting tools, planned hunting expeditions
1.5	mya	Hand axes, rudimentary language
750	kya	First use of fire
600	kya	Axes with handles
400	kya	Spears
150	kya	Grammatical language
120	kya	Burial of the dead
100	kya	First true humans
90	kya	First ornaments and jewellery
70	kya	*First Revolution*: cognitive thought
60	kya	Bow and arrow
50	kya	Counting with numbers
40	kya	Needles, musical instruments, simple dwellings
30	kya	Hand prints, cave painting and figurines
11	kya	*Second Revolution*: agriculture
10	kya	Dogs domesticated, first houses
8	kya	Ice Age retreats, cereals grown
7	kya	Copper smelting, wheeled vehicles
6	kya	Cattle, pottery, first cities and civilisations
5	kya	Writing, calendars, sailing ships
4	kya	Horses domesticated, religions established
3	kya	Stone Henge, Pyramids
2	kya	Long-distance trade routes in use
1200	BCE	The Trojan War
800–700	BCE	First recorded history and literature
600	BCE	The beginning of philosophy and politics
1500	CE	*Third Revolution*: science and technology
1950	CE	*Fourth Revolution*: information and virtual reality

3 What's on our Mind?

Blank slate, empiricism, rationalism, emotions, instincts, intuitions, the unconscious, culture.

O the mind, mind has mountains. *Gerard Manley Hopkins*

> *We live in two worlds, which our mind has evolved to integrate into a single reality.*

The mind at birth

When we look into our mind, what do we see? Is it a blank slate waiting to be inscribed by experience, or is the plot of our story already written there? We expect computer software to be programmed to do specific jobs, not to be empty, and our mind is similarly scripted in advance. When we scan the room as a baby, our brain is not buzzing with confusion, but primed with categories and instructions without which we can't make sense of the flood of incoming information.

Empiricists put the emphasis on the inputs: nothing can exist in our mind that is not first 'put to the test' through our senses. The only way we can know the taste of pineapple is by putting some in our mouth. This sounds basic enough, but it also accounts for our airiest mathematical abstractions, which go back to that moment when we first got our hands dirty in the sandpit. Our assumptions about cause and effect are the product of experience and memory, not theorising. We *expect* a stone to fall when we drop it, because that's what has always happened before.

Feral children raised by wolves or locked away by cruel parents tragically prove how much the mind needs stimulating input. Denied language and human contact, they grow up mute and unable to function socially. When rescued, they struggle to make up for all the lost love and culture of their childhood years, and often die before their time.

Behaviourist psychologists picked up on empiricist ideas. If our mind is the sum of our experiences, by changing our experiences, we can change our mind. This is good news if we are trying to break a bad habit or escape depression, but not if our thoughts are the targets of ideologues trying to fill our heads with what they think we should be thinking.

Rationalists don't deny the importance of sensory input, but focus instead on our capacity to make sense of it through a quality of mind called reason. The world overwhelms our brain with a chaotic flood of stimuli experienced up close and personal, constantly swirling into each other. Only reason enables us to categorise our perceptions, analyse them at one remove, and deduce rules that hold true across all situations. A stone always falls to the earth *because of* an invisible force called gravity.

Empiricists and rationalists are both right, but only half so. Empiricists are justified in pointing out that the beauty of the rainbow is created by our brain, but they are rash to claim that what lies outside sensory experience cannot be known, or is not worth knowing. Rationalists are correct in insisting that reason is necessary, but it is not always sufficient. Without imagination, we cannot join up our ideas or make sense of falling in love.

For life and the universe to be intelligible, we need sense and reason to work in harmony, because we cannot live a purely sensory existence, or comprehend the world by thought alone. The senses can sometimes deceive and logic can lull us into a false sense of security, as the well-fed turkey discovered on Christmas Eve.

Something on our mind

Some believe that our mind comes with memories of a previous life, others that it is empty, waiting to be filled up by experience. Biologists and cognitive scientists give us a more nuanced and complex picture of how we grow into minded individuals.

To make meaning, establish reliable knowledge and see what the eye cannot see, we need to be able to synthesise what we experience in the heat of each moment with a set of assumptions about the world that don't disappear when we shut our eyes. When we visit our doctor, we hope she has both a good fund of empirical experience so that she can recognise our symptoms, and a sound theoretical grasp of the latest advances in medicine. She is a fine example of how to turn theory into practice. Data, no matter how abundant, does not become knowledge until we convert it into appropriate interpretations and effective actions.

Evolution has given us a head start in this kind of mixed and balanced knowing. Our mind needs input, but it is also loaded by natural selection with some powerful cognitive programs. We are gifted a way of knowing without knowing how we know: up is higher than down, after follows before, hot is to cold as night is to day.

This precognition operates as a kind of mental glue, or cement of the universe. Experiments with babies as young as six months show that they look twice at events that defy their expectations. It is as if the laws of physics are already imprinted on the mirror of their minds.

Growing a mind

It takes most of our early years to form a mind because our brain has a lot of growing to do after birth, not settling down to its final configuration until our early twenties. In our first four years it undergoes a counterintuitive process called neural pruning, where neurons that are under-used are co-opted by busier parts of the brain, or wither away if left idle.

This explains why a French baby grows to sound 'naturally' French, while an English teenager learning French at school struggles to do so. If not stimulated in the early years, the neurons for learning French sounds fade away, or are put to other uses. The good news is that, whether French or English, we don't need any lessons in grammar while in the cradle. Being showered with the sounds of our native tongue is enough.

Our single brain could never invent language from scratch, but it doesn't need to. We are born into a language community and primed to extract meaning from the social grooming of chat. Through the faculty of imagination, our mind has the capacity to add something to experience, transforming modest input into rich output. The humblest peasant can become a great poet.

Our understanding of time and space also depends on the synergy of sense data and reason. In our early years, we reprise the cognitive journey of our ancestors.

Hunter gatherers tended to live in the moment: either there was prey or there was not. When they became farmers, they needed to evolve a concept of time that enabled them to see harvests as future rewards for past labours. By the same token, we find it hard as children to understand that we have to wait a whole hour before we can have that ice cream. At that age, an hour feels like an eternity.

It also takes us many years to broaden our concept of space. At first our street is the centre of the known world, just as, when the first maps appeared, cartographers always put themselves at the centre and made their own country the largest. Relying on sense-data alone gives us a very limited perspective on where we stand in relation to the vastness of the cosmos.

Emotional depths

Empiricism and rationalism are powerful theories for explaining how the mind works, but they are rather dry and useless without each other. Noting down everything we see and analysing its properties gives us no grounds for preferring one thing to another. For that, we need our emotions.

We did not evolve as a clever cortex perched on top of a prehistoric brain stem, reason lording it over raw sensory experience. We needed all of our brain to survive our long childhood on the savannah, and our 'primitive' brain still has a great deal to teach us, especially the amygdala, a tightly packed group of neurons tucked deep inside our brain which forms around six months of age.

From this brain region emanate our base emotions of fear and disgust, but it is a mistake to see our amygdala as an unruly part of our brain that we need to tame, or emotion as an inferior response when a superior one has failed. Our emotions can indeed lead us astray, urging us to donate a large sum to a national appeal for one sick child to have a life-saving operation while ignoring the more rational option of giving a smaller amount regularly to feed an unnamed starving family for a whole year.

This does not mean that our emotions are useless passions. They evolved to register changes in our bodily state, then *movivate* us to act. If we see a rhinoceros charging towards us, we run. We don't know *why* we are running, we just do. Only when we get to safety, our heart still racing, can we can deploy our 'thinking' neural networks to process what our emotion *means*. After all, we feel the same excitement when we jump out of a plane. In fact we chase this thrill purely *because* it gives us an adrenalin rush and a pumping heart.

In other words, we have the emotion first, then appraise what we are feeling. This is necessary because emotions don't come with automatic meanings. They are affected by the context of our experience, what we are expecting, who we're with, and our interpretation of it after the event.

They are also highly contagious, so it pays to understand how they work. Fear is not for instance the amygdala's only emotional flavour. It can also be the seat of love and hate, joy and despair. It doesn't 'decide' which one we get: *we* do, because our decisions are mediated through our consciousness.

Our amygdala registers an input and pumps adrenalin into our system, often before we have time to consciously 'clock' it. Our response to that input is filtered through a complex maze of pathways in the higher regions of our brain, the cortex and neocortex.

This slow-down gives us time to differentiate a stimulus from our feeling about it, saving us from throwing terrible-twos tantrums every time we don't get our own way. It allows us to refine our emotional responses as we grow, taking thought about what we feel and adding emotional tone to our reasoning.

Seen through the lens of evolution in deep time, our brain looks like a club sandwich. We share the bottom slice of bread with slugs and chickens, as our interface with raw experience. We hold the middle slice in common with all mammals, crammed with programs for feeding, communicating, reproducing and socialising. The top slice, our neocortex, is unique to our species, the 'thinking canopy' which expanded rapidly in our time as hunter gatherers on the savannah.

We should not allow this model of the mind to lure us into thinking that one part of our brain is smarter than another, or that reason is 'higher' than emotion. Nothing in our mind is so simple. It has evolved to work as a cooperative, not a hierarchy. For every decision we make, we need all of our brain fully functioning all of the time. We can't relegate emotion to lower down in the brain, as a kind of embarrassment when we are in company.

On the contrary, emotions evolved to direct us towards other people and to help us manage our social relations. They run all through our cortex and without them, we have no mechanism for preferring to treat people well or badly. Even our most 'logical' deductions are value-laden, because they emanate from our passion for coming to the right conclusion about anything. How else can we make a moral choice between donating our spare cash to charity or blowing it on a holiday?

THE STUPENDOUS STORY OF US

Evolutionary glitches

Understanding our brain from an evolutionary perspective helps us to realise that it is a Heath-Robinson contraption, not a state-of-the-art design. Each new bit has been clumsily bolted on to what was already there, like a bad house extension. We can't go back and alter the foundations.

This explains our craving for fat, salt and sugar. These goodies were rarely on offer on the savannah, so our ancestors grabbed them when they could. Our ability to gorge on them any time is at the root of our modern epidemics of obesity and heart disease.

The evolutionary glitches and gremlins go much deeper than that. One part of our brain insists that we're not racist, while another screams that immigrants are taking over our country. We make harsher decisions on an empty stomach, judge people unfairly on appearances, fill in any gaps in our thinking to avoid cognitive dissonance, and fabricate a self-narrative that only our friends can see through.

We don't do these things deliberately. On the savannah, a little bit of swagger and self-deception went a long way. 'Bigging up' our ego was our brain's tactic for getting us safely through another day.

Running on instinct

So are we just creatures of instinct? Not if we compare ourselves to a young antelope, which doesn't have time to practise getting to its feet and running away while hyenas are looking on hungrily. We take two years to learn how to stand up without falling over.

As babies we exhibit sucking, gripping, gag and startle reflexes, even the urge to hold our breath and swim under water, but the slow maturing of our neocortex through childhood leaves very little to pure instinct. We might be hardwired to jump at a loud noise, but not to believe in God, hate immigrants, crave alcohol or support Arsenal football club. These habits are not even prewired. They are learned, usually from those around us, and as such can be unlearned. Anger is a natural short-lived reaction if someone stands on our toes, but hatred of all people who wear size twelve shoes is an unnatural prejudice.

We might think we are born with an automatic fear of snakes, but as babies we show no fear of them, because our amygdala has not yet formed. As adults, we flinch reflexively if a snake lunges at us, but that's not the same as being in thrall to snake-phobia. By the laws of logic, we should also recoil from guns, fast cars and opioid painkillers, which are ten thousand times more likely to kill us. These were not however threats on the savannah, and evolution hasn't had time to make us 'instinctively' afraid of these new perils of the modern world.

Even motherhood is not instinctive. Women's bodies and brains are primed by oestrogen and oxytocin, but they still have to learn how to breast feed or be a good mother, especially if they weren't shown much love when they were young. As for men, fatherhood is like getting lost in a supermarket, until someone shows them the exit.

It makes more sense to consider human behaviour as conditioned by drives, not instincts. Hunger drives us to eat, but we don't have to eat on sight or gorge ourselves to death. Nor are we limbic puppets driven by our selfish genes to perform rampant sex at the sight of a potential mate. Sexual desire is a spinal reflex, but urges from our emotional centres have to pass through a labyrinth of cognitive processing before they are expressed as actions. Hermits can train themselves to go without food for weeks, and without sex completely.

Morality is therefore a cultivated art, not an automatic program. We are not born good or wicked but gradually, as experience inks its rules over the faint marks on the tracing paper beneath, we grow brain circuitry that can express empathy and foster good habits. We have to *learn* to be moral, with not a little help from parents, teachers, law enforcers and preachers without whom, as history shows, we might behave very badly indeed.

We can also opt for self-improvement by emulating those around us and practising the virtues. Sharing our sweets is hard the first time, but made easier when someone gives us one of their sweets next time. Passing the chocolates round is an ethical choice based on mutuality, with an obvious benefit and practical outcome. There is no need to debate our reasons.

Morality is a vaguer concept than ethics, but it still has its reasons, even in hard cases such as abortion and euthanasia. It has been variously grounded in divine command, public duty, mutual aid, gut feeling, evolutionary algorithm and the maximisation of good for the greatest number, but however approached, it is never a free for all.

Regardless of how our moral intuitions come to us, we always end up with the same core convictions, serving as objective facts in the spaces between us: striving for the greater good is right and harming each other is wrong. Slavery

THE STUPENDOUS STORY OF US

and infanticide are evil, and there is no world in which they could be good. We don't need mathematical calculation to reach this conclusion. It comes from much deeper down, embedded in the very ways we think and feel.

So how do we *know* that incest is wrong? The answer is complicated. Most of us say it doesn't *feel right* that a brother and sister should sleep together, even if they take precautions and keep it secret. Society agrees. Kinship systems have evolved over many generations to ensure brides and grooms come from different families, preferably from neighbouring villages. The dangers of in-breeding were well known, even though there was no knowledge of genetics. The fact that all cultures regulate marriage in this way hints at a universal moral grammar.

Relying on intuition

Does intuition serve us better than instinct? Some say that morality and the religious sense are based on intuition, but by that reckoning, we could add our sense of number, or our ability to read other people's minds when we talk to them. These are better seen as cognitive faculties programmed into us by evolution. Science and mathematics by comparison don't come to us so effortlessly, which is why we have to pore over them for long hours at school.

Intuition is often thought of as 'sixth sense' or 'gut feeling', a wisdom of the body that comes to us unbidden, a kind of thinking without thinking which gets us out of lots of scrapes. We can know without knowing how we know. It has been described as emotion-driven 'system one' or 'blink' thinking, designed to make us act first and ask questions later.

But knee-jerk reactions are seldom the best option, and hunches don't appear out of the blue. They are based on experiences that we have long forgotten, or knowledge that we have sublimated in our unconscious. Feeling uneasy about someone we have just met is based on dozens of memories of being too trusting in the past. We might not be consciously aware of them, but our brain has kept a careful record.

Over time it accumulates a vast fund of adaptive life-lessons, but it doesn't have the bandwidth to keep them all available all of the time, nor does it need to. They sit quietly in the lumber room of our mind, until some distant memory is stirred. How did things work out the last time we were in this fix? This slower 'system two' thinking allows us time to reflect, potentially saving us from making a fool of ourselves.

This is a wise precaution because intuitions are not infallible. To become knowledge, they must be put to the test. Despite our initial doubts, the person we at first feel negative about might turn out to be eminently trustworthy.

What goes on out of sight

Freud called the subterranean realm of our mind the *id*, below the radar of our wide-awake *ego*. He saw it as a dark place where, having seen something nasty in the woodshed, the trauma gets buried beyond the reach of our conscious mind. We don't want our fears, anxieties and failures erupting into our daytime affairs, so our mind lets them loose at night, in our dreams and nightmares.

He set up generations of therapists offering lengthy 'talk cures' aimed at helping anxious clients come to terms with their demons. But although Freud had a medical background, scientists remain very dubious about his idea of the unconscious. If its purpose is to hide itself from view, it makes us strangers to ourselves, and if it is mysterious, it cannot be studied empirically.

More controversially, he suggested that memories can lie buried for years, only to be triggered years later, but there is no evidence for this. The greater danger is that false memories can be implanted, which the brain convinces itself really happened.

Nevertheless, or perhaps because of this, his ideas about the unruly unconscious inspired a generation of writers to experiment with 'automatic writing', in which strange messages well up from some mysterious hinterland. It is more likely however that they were evoking images, thoughts and feelings already known to them but lost to their conscious mind.

Modern cognitive psychologists prefer to describe the ninety per cent of mental activity below the waterline as our non-conscious. Consciousness is phenomenal in the true sense of the word, a 'show' put on by our brain to alert our waking mind to what is happening right now. This is necessarily highly selective because there are thousands of functions going on inside us, from blood pressure to digestion, of which we are oblivious. These only 'appear on stage' if we feel faint or have a stomach ache.

Similarly, we make many of our daily decisions without knowing why. When we vote on election day, we think we're making a rational decision based on our analysis of the issues, but deep down we are casting our lot based on long-held gut feelings that we can barely put into words.

We need to remember that our mind is not a remote island, but part of the busy continent of society and culture, which exercise powerful influences on our thinking. Our feelings are not isolated operators, and our thoughts are never entirely free. From the moment we are born we absorb the folkways, attitudes and values of our peers and mentors. We think the thoughts, speak the words and travel the paths of millions of forebears. The past is always present, and there is no view from nowhere. It is culture that teaches us that, although a tomato is a fruit, we shouldn't put it in a fruit salad.

But we could if we wanted. Although much of what is in our mind is given to us, first by nature and second by nurture, we are free to analyse what we have learned, to question what we have been taught, and to unlearn what we feel is dragging us down. We can climb the mountains of our mind, in search of our own view from somewhere.

Layers of the Mind

This is only a model of the mind, not an explanation of our every thought or feeling.
In the brain and the mind, everything is connected to everything else all of the time.

Neocortex **modern human** plan the future extended consciousness	*200* *thousand* *years old*	*rationality* – reasoning outside space-time *intellect* – 'coolly' analysing *cognition* – thinking symbolically *drives* – overriding impulses
Cortex **mammalian** deal with the present non-conscious prompts	*120 million* *years old*	*anticipation* – predicting what comes next *emotion* – 'hotly' responding *arousal* – moving on quickly *intuitions* – relying on winning strategies
Brain stem **reptilian** remember the past body awareness	*300 million* *years old*	*attention* – focusing on stimuli *sensuality* – processing raw feels *nerves* – directing centrally *instincts* – reacting reflexively
Proto brain **earliest life forms** automated processes zero consciousness	*2 billion* *years old*	*defence* – protecting cell boundaries *energy* – finding food sources *regulation* – controlling metabolism *reproduction* – replicating copies

4 What stories do we tell about ourselves?

Story, twin realities, dualism, myth, time, art, imagination, new myths for a post-mythical world.

We are in between stories. The old story, the account of how we fit into it, is no longer effective. Yet we have not learned the new story.   *Thomas Berry*

> *Storytelling is a primary act of mind, and we flourish best when our new stories grow naturally out of our old.*

Living in twin realities

There are no stories in nature, only sequences of events, but to our human perception, we are psychonauts on a journey from birth to death. Our mind is a natural spinner of yarns, unifying our social experience into a joined-up narrative. When we see someone walking down the road, we automatically ascribe a personality, plot and purpose to the figure in the frame, because we cannot see the world as anything but story-shaped.

Shown oddments and fragments, our brain's instinct is to create a whole from so many parts. Given four random items, it is likely to fashion them into a story. It evolved as a pattern-seeking prediction device, intent on mapping reality and filling in any gaps. We have a blind spot in the middle of our vision, but we don't notice it because our brain completes the picture by default. For there to be closure and understanding, the inexplicable has to be explained.

This is why we crave beginnings and endings, especially for our own story. We can't relate to cosmic time, which is distant and impersonal, so we invent a human 'once upon a time' and project our own 'ever after'. The stars are merely giant balls of gas, but we give them human identities and mythological personalities.

We live in a world of matter, but materialism leaves us stranded in a world of things. For a life that matters, we need the 'I' perspective that only story can provide, helping us to feel we are going somewhere, grasp the mystery of being and protect ourselves from randomness.

Sir Thomas Browne, writing in the seventeenth century, was aware of our need for narrative. He compared us to a frog, born into one element but awaiting transformation into another. Confined in the watery womb, we anticipate our first lungful of air as a terrestrial spirit. Beginning as a conglomeration of atoms, we end as a collection of stories we tell about ourselves.

Sir Thomas Browne

1605–1682

Most scientists are materialists: what we see is what we get. The rest is fiction. Sir Thomas's experiences as a doctor taught him that mind and body are not so easily separated. We are the sum total of the stories we tell each other. Modern therapists agree.

Story-making is our brain's response to living in twin realities, and our mind's refusal to be reduced to physics. Outside of us we see a world of stuff, over which we have little control, but inside our head we feel that we are directing our own movie, projected onto the screen of our mind. We are imprisoned in our body, but our imagination is free to roam.

René Descartes, writing at the same time as Sir Thomas on the other side of the English Channel, captured this dualism in his formula 'I think, therefore I am'. Our body ties us to a time and place, but the 'clear and distinct ideas' of our mind transport us to a universal reality. He was a mathematician, so he should know.

Mind from matter

Most scientists are unhappy with this split between matter and mind. The mind may *feel* omnipotent, but it is firmly grounded in brain events. A mind-changing drug, bang on the head or coma leave us in no doubt that mind states ride on the coat tails of brain chemistry. In the case of death, when the brain stops functioning, the mind disappears completely.

The most common reconciliation between body and mind is compatibilism: while the brain is functioning, mind will be present, and when minding is in evidence, there must be a brain driving it. A coin can't have tails without a head.

Another explanation for non-material mind is emergence. Somewhere along the gradient of the complexity of life, there is a qualitative step change towards a new way of being in the world, a phase transition that cannot be explained merely by the physics and chemistry of the parts down below. Regardless of how it comes about, we end up with several ways of knowing, each telling us a different kind of story about the matter of our brain and the life of our mind.

It remains a great mystery how material 'brain stuff' can generate the immaterial sense of 'what it's like to be me', but we should not be surprised that evolution has shaped our mind to explore every avenue in its quest for meaning. The modern quest for the Theory of Everything, the Holy Grail of physicists, is at once a scientific quest, a work of art and a search for an overarching story. If it exists at all, it can only be as a unification of all our little stories into one grand narrative.

The power of myth

Our brain is an engine that answers to two sovereign masters, Mythos and Logos. Logos looks for 'logical' reasons, but on the savannah these were in short supply. Mythos answered a deeper need for explanation: the boom of the thunder is the voice of an angry god. Denied access to modern physics textbooks, our ancestors had no choice but to explain strange events in terms they could understand.

Myth, like religion, addresses profound questions of life, sex and death. It therefore played a much greater role in the evolution of mind than its present status as make believe and fairy tale. As early as 1590, in the painting 'The Fall of Icarus', Pieter Breugel reduces to a footnote in the background Icarus's dramatic crashing to earth, while normal life goes on obliviously in the foreground.

We cannot however doubt the ways in which the myth of Icarus retains its resonance today, nor can we ignore its powerful message not to fly too close to the sun. Like all the great myths, it echoes down the millennia because it still speaks to a deep inner need.

Every culture has contributed to a collective memory of seminal stories which mark crucial refinements in human consciousness, about love, loyalty, evil and dying a good death. These give us not profane, historical and literal truths, but sacred, psychological and allegorical ones. Adam and Eve are not real people, but archetypes of all of us. They teach us in symbolic form how to become self-aware, understand our limitations, and shoulder the burden of experience. They give us a vision of who we have been, and who we want to become.

Life itself is a mythical journey which we punctuate with rites of passage: our birthday, first day at school, first love, first job. Our setbacks too have to be seen in the frame of gradual self discovery and growing resilience in the face of suffering. Our dreams are private myths, made more powerful when shared as public narratives to live by. Regardless of whether the Bible or Odyssey are grounded in real historical events, we still read them today for what they have to teach us about pride, humility, courage, honour and the determination to succeed.

Myth infuses every aspect of our thinking and being, starting with our notion of time. Cosmological time doesn't care whether we are here to see it tick by or whether the Earth reverses its spin. Clock time is merely tedious, the daily brushing of our teeth and inexorable descent to the grave. Only spiritual time can redeem our days from deadly tedium and make the thought of our eventual death bearable. We crave the true myth that we are purposefully engaged in making a fairer and kinder world.

Our addiction to mythmaking can however leave us exposed. Our brain, primed to sequence events as past, present or future, helps us to integrate random experiences into an ordered narrative, but this can render us vulnerable to oversimplification. We expect news stories to reduce complex issues to a single catchy headline, because this saves us the effort of digging any deeper or considering alternative accounts.

In similar vein we look to history books to give us the 'causes' of events, even though they are impossible to disentangle. We people their pages with clean-cut heroes and villains, overlooking the fact that each is a troubling mix of good and bad. We carve the past into periods, ages and dynasties, but these are mere labels of convenience, masking endless false starts and premature endings. We rebrand the past according to present tastes and priorities.

Countries carefully curate their national story, crafting the image they want to present to the world. We do the same with our own memories, writing our lives backwards by privileging those moments that fit the story we want to tell about ourselves, while blanking those that don't. In this sense, memory is not about the past at all, but a present device that we use to manipulate the future.

We take causality as a given, written deep into nature, but that forces us to see time as an arrow flying irreversibly in one direction. We can't otherwise establish cause and effect, tell stories or make sense of anything that happens. 'If … then …' sequential reasoning governs our understanding of human nature: they got divorced *because* they fell out of love. Without such thinking, we could not make the step up to scientific method: the tides change *because* the moon's gravity tugs at the world's oceans.

Natural story tellers

Lived time is the heartbeat of the stories we tell, which in turn define who we are and how we interpret the world. Our ancestors regaled each other with tales around the campfire at night. Today, novelists, film directors and designers of computer games take advantage of our obsession with story by tinkering with timelines, but they always revert to default: there was a beginning, there is a middle, and there will be an end.

News editors know that, so long as they grab our attention with a story, we'll follow the narrative to the end. Science writers understand that, as in the title of this book, everything from the opening scenes of the cosmos to the finale of evolution is best told as a story.

Stories offer us a journey to our own interior. Research shows that different types of story activate particular parts of our brain, helping us to grow cognitively and emotionally as we adopt avatars of ourselves: heroes and villains, helpers and tricksters, winners and losers. Through these we discover thoughts and feelings we didn't know we were capable of entertaining, and learn what it might feel like to be in situations we will never experience.

As we enter the shared space of other minds, we become more empathic. Theory of mind, or the ability to read each other's thoughts, was a vital skill for our ancestors, desperate to keep the peace in tight-knit groups. We are fascinated to know what makes others tick. Over half of our daily chat is taken up in gossiping our way through the exploits of our neighbours.

To this end, our stories are full of heroes who are not zombies but self-motivated characters with distinct personality traits. They have a thousand faces,

THE STUPENDOUS STORY OF US

and the stories we weave around them reflect our aspirations and values. They teach us how to humble ourselves ready for the quest and face down our demons. By taking us out of ourselves and letting us walk in their shoes, they give us time to grow bigger and wiser.

The fact that we can revisit their stories over and over, responding to them on different levels each time, alerts us to the fact that their meaning is never fixed, but constantly changing at the tip of our consciousness. Their costumes may change, but the underlying moral messages are constant, tapping us in directly to the cumulative wisdom of mankind.

This is overwhelmingly positive, because stories that encourage cruelty or selfishness do not get passed on. Amoral stories disconcert us and immoral ones leave us terrified, but good stories are morality tales which assure us that all will eventually be well. In them core truths are consistently confirmed: we owe each other a duty of care, our sins will find us out, virtue will be rewarded, and the greater good, no matter how many forces mass against it, will eventually prevail.

Trafficking in symbols

We couldn't indulge in story or art at all without the ability to traffic in symbols. We don't just see, we *see as*, one thing standing in for another. Scratches on a stone can represent lunar cycles, number of kills or just a fascination with pattern. Symbolisation, or throwing two ideas together to make a novel combination, allows us to endow ordinary objects with extraordinary significance: the mountain is the dwelling place of the gods and, more playfully, the moon is a balloon.

Symbolic art has been part of our story from the beginning. Daubed rocks, carved effigies, decorated tools and crafted jewellery have been found going back to our Homo erectus forebears. In cave paintings discovered in Europe and Asia, dating from up to thirty-five thousand years ago, we see outlines of animals of such grace and power that Picasso took inspiration from them. They were not intended as 'public' art as we understand it today, but were hidden in the dark, viewable only by flickering flame, which probably brought the animals alive.

We will never know what was in the mind of the cave painters, but in their chimaeras of half-men and half-beasts we feel our mind quickening in the evolutionary womb. It is likely that the art was linked to fertility cults, as veneration for the animals, calling up their spirits ready for the next hunt, or apologising for having to kill them.

Intriguingly, few people appear in the paintings, and the caves seem to have been abandoned after a few thousand years, suggesting that our ancestors felt safe enough to move out into the open, building the first semi-permanent dwellings. They took with them their fascination with sacred icons and graven images.

Today we see only the afterglow of their original mythical vision. Modern columns, arches, spires and skyscrapers are not just shadows of the huge temples, idols, frescoes and mausoleums of the past, they are also tributes to the magnificent structures of nature. Mimesis is the urge to imitate and improve upon what we see. It is the basis of culture, each generation building on the achievements of its forebears.

We see in children's art the urge to copy what they see and create anew through the power of imagination. Plato believed that fiction and art are dangerous lies, mixing fact and fantasy, deceiving us with illusion. Psychologists now agree that make believe is not only harmless, it teaches us what we *can* believe. In that sense, play is essential for firming up our grasp on truth and reality. Putting the laws of nature on hold temporarily is our way of consolidating what we know and exploring what we don't yet know.

Seeking a new story

Underlying time, story and imagination is a foundation myth subscribed to by both Sir Thomas and Monsieur Descartes: there is a reality beyond what appears to our senses. We see faces in the clouds or in the embers of a fire. Such hallucinations might have been our first gods. Our ancestors were animists. When a tree swayed in the breeze, it mattered little to them whether the leaves were pushing the air or vice versa. The whole of nature was alive and the world was full of demons.

The spirits inhabiting the beasts, rivers, mountains and forests were first seen and felt as female earth deities. The earliest figurines are of the female form, probably used as fertility symbols. Invested with the great mystery of childbearing, women ruled the roost for most of our evolutionary childhood.

This changed as our ancestors became settled farmers. Once the big game had been hunted out, they were forced to dig and harvest, tame and herd. The fertility cults, rituals and sacrifices associated with hunting slowly faded, and land ownership became a male affair. Earth spirits gradually became sky gods, a transition reflected in the myth cycles of the ancient world. Demeter gradually gave way to Zeus, and Logos started to oust Mythos.

Sir Thomas and Monsieur Descartes are now seen as the last hurrah of the twin realities of body and mind, and the final lament of the idea of a transcendent fifth dimension. It is a world we have lost. In our sceptical and materialist times we dismiss the 'grand narrative' of a numinous reality that sustained the human spirit for so many millennia.

But we still need myths to live by. Science is now our materialist story and emblem of rationality, but science alone, having discredited our old legend, cannot single-handedly give us a new one. The formula of hypothesis, experiment, review and test again has given us intellectual tools and technological powers that our ancestral pantheon could only imagine, and for the first time in four billion years the future of our planet is in the hands of one species. We have become our own gods.

But to answer Gauguin's questions, we still need the old stories. We have to make sense of the arc of our life, we want to understand other minds, we enjoy losing ourselves in the land of fable, we turn to art for inspiration, we yearn to express ourselves creatively. Our attitude to religion has altered significantly, but our spiritual need for meaning and purpose has not gone away. Telling our own stories helps us to find our inner voice and make sense of our thoughts and feelings. Immersing ourselves in great stories told by others shows us better versions of ourselves.

We cannot rely on science alone to humanise us because, after two hundred years of unrelenting materialism, it has come full circle. Quantum theory reveals that matter is not so solid after all, but a whizz of spinning particles. We can't deduce future from past states, and when we step into the current to observe the water we alter its flow. This might turn out to be the ultimate *mysterium tremendum* which could restore our relationship with the world we so casually exploit: we are part of what we observe.

Little wonder that myths in every cultural tradition warn us of the dangers of overweening power. We are all potentially a Midas or a Frankenstein. When we look across the world, we realise we haven't been particularly good at replacing our ancestors' mythical understanding of the world with stories that are better, or as spiritually nourishing. Materialism, communism, capitalism, globalism, nationalism and secularism come with their own golems and gremlins.

Carl Jung reminded us that, while it is easy to jettison myths whose resonance has drained away, it is much harder to work out what spiritual need they served. It is even more difficult to create new myths that sustain us and write new stories that unite us. He realised that Monsieur Descartes still has a story to tell. Sir Thomas surely agreed, remarking that 'We carry within us the wonders we seek around us'.

5 Who are we?

Self, saving face, identity, individuality, traits, personality, character, virtue ethics, critics of the self.

I am large, I contain multitudes. *Walt Whitman*

> *If the self is a trick of the brain, it is the cleverest act of conjuring we will ever experience.*

The self in the mirror

Every story needs a narrator, but who do we see when we look in the mirror? 'Look at things from *my* point of view' is merely our ego talking, not the interpersonal self mirrored in the eyes of others. Like Narcissus, are we are in love with our own reflection? Is our unshakeable sense of 'this is me' as insubstantial as a mirage in the desert? Are we helplessly locked into our 'I' perspective on the world? Is our pulsating sense of self merely a trick of our brain?

Psychologists credit us with several 'working' selves, aimed variously at looking after number one, remembering who we are, finding a mate, keeping our friends and getting on in life, so we shouldn't be surprised if our self feels neither fixed nor singular. Holding all of our subselves together in the cut and thrust of life is as big a challenge as developing a strong frame to support our body.

We sport a public self, which is open to the world. In many respects, there can be no private self without other minds and bodies to engage with, our sense of who we are taking shape in the spaces between us. If we're lucky, we might arrive at a degree of self knowledge, though getting to understand our innermost self may still elude us after a lifetime of searching, even if we keep a secret diary.

This is because there is no 'pure self' behind the public facade. The self is encumbered with layers of social expectation and performance. We evolved as highly gregarious creatures, a large part of our brain devoted to monitoring our status in the group. Some liken the self to a work of art. It is, but we are not the creators. That we owe to other minds, though we rarely fathom their influence on our life.

When we walk into a room, we are highly conscious of who is looking at us. Our eyes scan the room for someone who recognises us, or who might be of like mind. Psychologists call this the 'looking glass self'. When we say we feel self-conscious, what we really mean is that we are conscious of others looking at us.

In company we put on a show or modulate our self in relation to our audience. When mingling with others, whether at home, at work, standing in a queue or attending a wedding, we follow a script appropriate to that situation. In each case people assign a role to us, and we rarely disappoint them.

This isn't insincerity, more a case of staying in character. We have to manage our public persona, which is not the same as our personality. *Persona* was originally a mask used by Roman actors, their voice emerging from behind a facade. The only time we allow our mask to drop is when we are alone, and sometimes not even then. Occasionally we surprise ourselves by adding another act to our repertoire without knowing we had it in us. We get away with it because everyone else is playing the same game.

Our face serves as our mask. We talk about being two-faced, putting on a brave face and facing our enemies down. Our success in society depends on our ability to give others room to save face, especially in front of others. If we humiliate them, they will be 'in our face' forever and a day.

The undivided self

Philosophers have long debated whether the self comes before or after experience, but from a personal perspective, for as long as we draw breath and are compos mentis, our sense of *this is me* feels so empirical and immediate that we take it completely on trust. It is an enduring reality that comes with the territory, serving as our anchor in the shifting currents of life, so 'common sensical' that even when we're shown its fickleness, we still can't see through its charade.

For a start, the *physical* basis of our self is anything but constant. Every few years, with the exception of our teeth enamel, all the atoms in our body are traded in for others. When we are ninety however, we still feel the same person as the nine year old child in our photograph collection. Our memories give us continuity of identity, even though we put them temporarily on hold while we sleep and we rewrite them as we age. Take away our memories, as happens under anaesthesia, or in dementia, and our self evaporates. Our attitudes, values, feelings and beliefs no longer have any habitation or name.

Brain transplants and teleportation prompt interesting questions about the relation of our self to our body. We call ourselves individuals, on the basis that the self is un-dividable. Occasionally the brain hemispheres of epileptic patients are surgically separated to prevent life-threatening seizures, potentially creating two persons where there was one. In Siamese twins, who might have two heads on one body, or vice versa, isolating the 'self' of each is problematic. If we are vaporised and sent halfway across the galaxy, or our brain is downloaded to a machine, where do 'we' end up?

The persistence and indivisibility of the self is essential for moral, legal and political purposes: the sanctity of the self is inviolable, our rights are non-negotiable and we are sole keepers of our own bodies. We cannot be coerced against our will, denied due process of law or imprisoned without cause.

But rights entail responsibilities. Regardless of how much we feel we change with the passing years, we are still accountable in our third age for the crimes we committed as a young person, as we see in the hunting down of war criminals after many decades. When we're in the dock, no matter how many identities or name-changes we have adopted in the meantime, we can't palm off our guilt on a part of us that died several years ago.

We are intimately and inextricably attached to our name, identity and signature. If someone steals who we are by hacking into our computer, or compromises our good name, we feel existentially threatened. The first thing authoritarian regimes do to prisoners of conscience is to strip them of their name, thereby reducing them to the status of non-persons. We dread anonymity or being left to rot in an unmarked grave.

Our sense of self emerges very early. As babies we soon learn where our bodies end, and other bodies begin. Even an octopus knows not to wrap itself round one of its own tentacles. By age one, we recognise ourselves in a mirror, and by age four, we have attitudes, beliefs, opinions and, as our parents are well aware, a will of our own.

In the nursery we slowly organise our internal chatter into public language, talking to ourselves as we play and using words to exchange ideas with others. We can now begin to write the story of our autobiographical self, a human comedy with ourselves in the starring role: we can best our enemies, find the golden fleece and return home victorious.

Together language and culture form a symbolic web which shapes our perception of the world. At its centre is the assumption of a sovereign self, constantly changing, but so slowly that not even our friends notice. Without it we could not learn 'reflexive' morality founded on self-control and self-reliance. We could never give our 'self' a good talking to or commune with our own thoughts on a solitary walk through the woods.

Getting to know ourselves

We've been walking upright for millions of years, but our sense of a self journeying alone through the world to a destination unknown has taken much longer to evolve. The heroes of Homer's epics feel guided in their actions by hearing the voice of a god in their head. Characters in the Bible see themselves more as obedient servants of God than as free agents. In the classical world, being an individual comes second to avoiding the retribution of fate.

Slowly however, thought and emotion combine to create the feeling of an inner self navigating its way through increasingly complex choices. Our sense of freedom, enhanced or diminished, can be lived out through the dilemmas faced by the avatars of our imagination.

Polonius's advice

'To thine own self be true', urges Polonius to his son in 'Hamlet'. But what if the self is unknowable, a fiction, an illusion or a trick of the brain?

By the Middle Ages, cultural changes begin to shape our modern sense of self. The troubadours sing openly of the delights of romantic love and the pleasures to be enjoyed in private experience. We can now read silently to ourselves, not be lectured to en masse in church. Encouraged by Martin Luther's declaration, 'Here I stand', we can choose our religion as a matter of personal conviction.

Small technological changes start to make a difference too. Sleeping and ablutions can be performed in private behind closed doors. We can sit on our own chair, not have to squeeze up on a bench. We can study our reflection in the mirror that we can now afford to have in our home.

In Renaissance art we begin to see rounded individuals, not figures in a flat tableau. We detect an idiosyncratic smile on the face of the Mona Lisa. The ability to paint perspective with a vanishing point allows us to explore a personal 'point of view' which lies at the heart of the human condition. By the time we get to Shakespeare, we are treated to a real quickening of consciousness as characters deliver complex soliloquies, pulling back the curtains on their hidden selves and voicing thoughts they have not yet heard themselves say.

Developing character

Alongside these historical shifts there were increasingly subtle attempts to catalogue the self in the form of character types with strong individual traits. Why are some of us charismatic leaders while others are submissive followers? Are we born this way, or does life make us thus?

An early attempt at explaining personality was the theory of humours, based on different mood-controlling fluids coursing through our veins. We still talk of being in a bad humour, or of melancholy and sanguine types. Another popular theory was the astrological signs of the zodiac: you're a fiery Scorpio, I'm a calm Aquarius. Many of us still check our horoscope each week.

Modern psychology hasn't taken us much further in getting to grips with what makes us tick, merely changed the terminology. We are stereotyped as extroverts or introverts, conformists or rebels, givers or takers, thinkers or doers. Biology fares little better, suggesting that personality is determined by genes or body shape. Thin people are neurotic, fat people are jolly. If we're open, moody, trustworthy, outgoing or downright miserable to be with, it's because we have inherited these traits from our parents.

There is much confusion between emotion, mood and character type. Darwin identified six emotions that are programmed into us by evolution, common to all cultures: joy, distress, anger, fear, surprise and disgust. These however are default reactions, not hallmarks that guarantee our sincerity. For a start, although they are felt personally, they are generally triggered by other people. Another complication is that each of us has different 'set points': you might be disgusted by the smell of damp dogs, but I love it.

So what about moods? We say things like 'she's a very moody person', but moods do not equate to character types either. We can alter our mood by sipping a hot drink on a cold day, or taking something stronger. We can be generally a positive person, but have an 'off' day. We can feel in a bad mood when we wake up, but find that we perk up by lunchtime.

Psychometric tests are formulated to label who 'we' are. Employers set great store by them, but clinical psychologists are not so sure. Most of us undermine them by giving the answers we think will get us the job. Not so, say the designers of the tests. You hardly know yourself. The real you can be known only from the outside, by people like us. If the tests have a value at all, it is in showing us not our strengths, which we're already good at. What we need to work on is our weaknesses, which is a question of character.

'Character' originally meant a stamp of proof, not as a mark we cannot erase but as a moral habit that we can cultivate. Virtue ethics is based on the belief that character goes deeper than a few ticks on our job application. It bypasses the notion of morality as abstract rules and focuses on achieving the greater good, not in some grand sense, but in the little practical acts of kindness that we can perform a thousand times a day, if we have schooled ourselves to act this way.

Virtue ethics does not assume that we are born good, bad, or saddled forever with fixed character traits. We are not at the whim of every passing fancy, but active agents in becoming more considerate and mindful. If a friend tells us we are behaving inconsiderately, we can learn to change, one small step at a time. This will feel hard at first, but gradually come more naturally. Without this open prospect there is no hope for the delinquent teenager, gambling addict, prisoner on parole, or partner who regularly forgets birthdays and anniversaries.

The disappearing self

In the West the concept of the self is fundamental to our idea of personal growth. Without it there can be no learning by the light of experience, which is the one thing we feel we can trust. When we're young, our teachers believe that they can enrich our inner life and cultivate our 'best self'. As we age, our mind turns to our finitude: it dawns on us that the base metal of the self that we have spent so long turning into gold is not as immortal as we thought.

Partly to avoid such existential dread, Eastern philosophers have approached the self very differently. Meditation is aimed not at realising the self, but escaping its distractions and anxieties. The Buddha taught that when we introspect we see nothing stable or substantial, only temporary ripples on the surface of our mind. When we say 'I' am offended, we are kidding ourselves. There is no 'I' to *be* offended, only passing feelings.

Postmodern theorists agree with this verdict, but for different reasons. All we see is signs, never the realities behind the signs. The world we are conscious of is a false one, largely a concoction of our social media feeds. We need not fret about who we 'are' today, because tomorrow we will 'be' a different person.

Cognitive scientists raise troubling questions about the neural foundations on which we base our sense of self. Which parts of our vaunted unitary self are sheared off in out-of-body experiences, hypnosis, schizophrenia, delirium, virtual reality body-swaps, phantom limb syndrome and vegetative states, and where do they disappear to?

We might feel that we are watching a single movie on the screen of our mind, but when neuroscientists scan our brain to locate the place where 'we' sit eating popcorn, they find that the auditorium is empty. There is no 'core' self, only shifting electrochemical patterns.

All we get to 'see' is what is given to our conscious awareness by our non-conscious, just enough to serve the needs of the present moment, amounting to no more than a minimal feed of passing phenomena. The mind is flat, and any sense of depth is a trick of the brain.

Dissociative Identity Disorder (DID), which used to be called multiple personality disorder, exposes the fragility of the neural networks that underpin our certainty about who we are. Children who are regularly abused often depersonalise themselves, creating as a defence a secondary self capable of watching the cruelty being inflicted on their primary self from a distance. Some DID sufferers lay claim to up to a dozen distinct 'selves'.

Social psychologists deliver the killer blow to the myth of a sovereign self. It is a fabrication, a story written backwards. We are giddy things, arch-deceivers that make things up as we go along, biddable and shallow. Our sense of being a free agent controlling thought and action is an illusion, admittedly a grand one, but still a work of our imagination.

THE STUPENDOUS STORY OF US

And yet here we are, reading these words, caring about questions like this, harbouring our secrets, seeking a nourishing life narrative, wanting to live a good life, trying to make a difference for others. We may never get to know our self fully, but we are convinced of its truths, even though they lie too deep to be expressed.

It is the only self we have, the part of us that was set growing as a seed in our child's mind and that we spend a lifetime feeding and watering. It is the self that suffers, fights back and knows that one day it will die. It is the self that we hope people will miss when they say goodbye to us at our funeral.

6 How sapiens are we?

Intelligence, gene-culture evolution, symbolisation, sexual selection, reason, irrationality, eugenics, IQ testing, potential, smart thinking, genius.

It's not how smart you are that matters, what really counts is how you are smart. *Howard Gardner*

> *Being smart means knowing when our cleverness is leading us astray.*

Getting smart

As tellers of our own tale we consider ourselves smart, but when we look closely we realise that smartness is spread throughout nature, expressed in particular ecological niches. Trees use their root systems as connected underground brains, communicating with each other and sharing resources. Spiders shape their webs as funnels, trapdoors, tunnels, orbs and nets to catch their chosen prey. Birds know how to navigate vast distances to the very upland meadow where they were born.

Collective intelligence takes smartness up a notch, starting in the insect world. One ant could not survive on its own, but two ants begin to make a colony or super-organism. Bees perform choreographed dances back at the hive to tell fellow workers how to make a beeline to a good pollen find.

For dogs in their packs, monkeys in their troops and dolphins in their schools, the evolutionary driver of their smartness is the complexity of their social life. They cooperate when it suits them, but they also keep secrets from each other, bearing grudges when they sense that trust has been broken. But solitariness can build intelligence too. Octopuses, even though they live most of their lives alone, remember the faces of individual divers.

In the wild, chimpanzees display great cunning to get food or sex, use sticks or stones as simple tools, and show a degree of empathy. In captivity they have been taught to communicate with humans by sign language. They attain levels of intelligence we would expect of a two-year old child, but do not progress beyond this point.

Chimps are so close to us genetically that some campaign for them to be granted legal status as 'persons'. They are certainly self-aware, but their survival in the wild does not demand full symbolic thought, the mental facility that allows us to see one thing as another. We inhabit a complex symbolic order of words, signs, taboos and values. We don't just think, we *think with* categories of likeness and difference, past and future, good and bad.

Chimps are clever at specific things, and we need to treat them ethically, but they are strangers to our social and cognitive worlds. Lack of language and inability to multitask prevents them from engaging in full cultural learning, which is our most transformative feature.

Selected for culture

To a degree enjoyed by no other animal, we are the beneficiaries of a powerful combo called gene-culture evolution. Our genes get us off to a good start in life, giving us easy mastery over core skills. We don't have to think about how to digest our food, put one word after another or walk on two legs, albeit after a few stumbles.

But being a fully functioning human being requires a great deal more than a few automatic neural programs and motor skills. Some species of animal abandon their young to chance the moment they are born, but we need a mother, an extended family, a well developed sense of empathy, a long childhood and a supporting culture to become sapiens. As the African proverb goes, it takes a village to raise a child. We owe everything we do and know to others, most of whom we have never met.

As well as inheriting a cognitive toolkit for fixing problems as they arise, we also need the ability to pass our knowledge on to the next user, usually with embellishments. At birth we are self-programmable, but our software is useless without massive downloads of interacting with others, being shown how to make things and learning how to behave appropriately in any given situation. We experience this as the embrace of human culture, which is smarter than any one individual could ever be.

Natural selection might have prioritised the genes for thousands of generations, but culture was also quietly shaping our biology in radical ways. Growing up in cooler climes with less sunlight, cereal growers and cattle farmers passed to their descendants genes for fairer skin, blue eyes and lactose tolerance, while those in tropical zones retained darker skins, brown eyes and allergies to dairy products.

The accidents of our geography and history also shaped our personality, or what we call human nature. The invention of the human family and discovery of paternity made males less aggressive towards each other and more protective of their offspring, allowing more young to survive. Our brain architecture was also steadily modified. As language and number skills accumulated, our brain needed to develop grammars and thinking patterns to accommodate them.

In other words, through the long millennia of our evolutionary childhood, culture was constantly feeding back to our genes, making us more tolerant of others, more psychologically complex and cognitively smarter. Also, passing on the rich fund of cultural knowledge promoted two key human traits, unique in nature: learnability and teachability. Not only did the young need a brain that could soak up knowledge as easily as their mother's milk, the old had to perfect techniques for serving it up in digestible chunks.

Genes are written in a universal code, but culture is expressed locally. The next generation needs to be taught how to extract the toxins from this particular plant, which type of tree provides the best timber for making a canoe, how to catch a seal when the sea is iced over. As Scott of the Antarctic discovered on his fated expedition, this kind of local knowhow can be the difference between life and death.

Modern creature comforts make it easy for us to forget the hard lessons that culture is built on. Were we to find ourselves stranded after a shipwreck, we would have no idea how to catch prey, skin it or light a fire to cook it. Culture is fragile, linked by delicate threads that are easily broken. White colonists were taken aback by the tough living conditions of Tasmanian Aborigines in the nineteenth century, who had lost many cultural skills after being separated from mainland tribes for ten thousand years. Merely staying alive was a real struggle for them.

Transmission of cultural knowhow is the secret of our success as a species, so it is no surprise that learning it and teaching it stimulated the growth of particular intelligences. To be truly smart, we need not only to process things logically but also to visualise the contents of each other's minds. We talk disparagingly of monkeys 'aping' each other, but in fact we are the true masters of imitation. We don't just follow the latest fashion craze, we also intuit the intention behind the act.

To learn anything we need insight, or the ability to see into the mind of the person teaching us. This is the great gift of human culture.

Cognitive revolution

Human intelligence reached its zenith after a series of mutations in our brain that were complete between seventy and a hundred thousand years ago. There was no sudden arrival of new genes. Our cognitive revolution was brought about by gradual adaptations which gave us new ways of processing information, networking ideas and imagining the future.

Our brain size had doubled over a million years before, but it wasn't the addition of grey matter in the cortex that clinched it. It was the reorganisation in the neocortex or 'new brain' of white matter, so-called because its axons or nerve fibres are covered by fatty myelin sheaths which speed up their ability to make associations and connections.

Neural potential was also boosted by the arrival of specialised 'higher thinking' spindle-shaped cells, though they are also found in other great apes, elephants and whales. In our case these more sophisticated smart-bots transformed our cognitive capacities, paving the way for enhanced understanding of time, space and language. If we are to consider ourselves unique or special in any way, we owe it to these super-neurons, and the way they are ever more subtly configured as we grow.

Symbolisation allowed us to represent thought in the abstract. A few scratches on a stone could now carry a message to another mind, overcoming the barriers of space and time. The past could now live in the present and the future could be planned.

Logic enabled us to reverse our thought, tracing it back to its sources, capitalising on the past as usable knowledge. Chains of causal reasoning allowed for if-then thinking, enhancing our power over nature: *if* we put tree trunks under this boulder, *then* we can lever or roll it to a new location. It is this kind of 'joined-up thinking' we rely on to recognise a bad argument when we hear one.

Alongside these new ways of thinking a dynamic additional device was slowly taking shape, piggybacking on the same neural software: verbal language. We can't say language *caused* the big brain or an explosion in intelligence, but alongside tool-making and social manoeuvring, it boosted our smartness exponentially. It enabled us to manipulate thought, exploit new ideas, bring the future into the present and bridge the spaces between us.

Selecting for reason

Animals by and large are limited to the environments in which they evolve, but we are a 'weed species' that can adapt to any soil. On the subtropical savannah we were not apex predators, but our powerful combination of genes and culture enabled us to colonise the steamy jungles, scorched deserts or icy wastes. No longer the hunted, we became the hunters.

The contemporary migrant crisis demonstrates how intelligence is the ability to know what to do when we don't know what to do. If smartness is about staying alive, an orphaned street urchin living on her wits in a bombed-out city is much more likely to survive than an educated high school child living without challenge in a leafy suburb. Those who risk their lives making perilous sea crossings to escape poverty and persecution are testimony to the resilience and resourcefulness of our ancestors.

Natural selection favours the smart and the flexible in both genders, but sexual selection is at work too. She wanted more than brawn, and he wanted more than buxomness. She looked for more than macho flirting, and he knew that she could be as strong, determined and sexually adventurous as he was. Each was honing each other's intelligence as much as hunting for good genes. Surviving hunter-gatherer societies show that powerful females are the norm, and caring males are no new thing. A society that ignores this legacy is reducing its cognitive capital by fifty per cent, not to mention its emotional real estate.

We call ourselves sapiens, or wise and reasonable. Reason derives from *ratio*, or the ability to relate one idea to another. The sequential nature of logical thinking permits us to use reason as a cognitive lever. Something cannot be what it is not, and nothing can happen without a reason. I think *therefore* I am. As far as we know, no other animal is capable of building staircases of thought in this way.

As well as logic however, we rely on reason to make us thoughtful, in the sense of offering a measured response, avoiding knee-jerk responses and conspiracy theories. Only reason can make us aware of the blind spots in our own thinking.

Justice and the law pride themselves on their ability to separate reason from passion, and principle from prejudice. No matter how many examples of unreason we come across every day, and there are plenty, there is never any excuse for behaving irrationally or unreasonably.

In the seventeenth century Francis Bacon tried to banish what he called 'idols of the mind', which hold us back from thinking clearly: we are easily duped by our perceptions, we use language loosely, we are sucked in by tradition, we believe what others tell us, we don't look at what is actually in front of us. These gremlins, he insisted, are the enemies of reason and science.

Such thinking cleared many obstacles, and within a hundred years, after centuries of domination by religious teaching, Enlightenment philosophers were declaring that reason could solve all our problems, not just of the head but also of the heart.

Their trumpeting of rationality set many free from superstitious thinking, but by the late eighteenth century there was an upsurge of revolutionary ardour, nationalistic fervour and romantic passion, unleashing a blood tide in some countries.

It turned out that overlooking the role of emotion in human affairs presented a dangerously narrow view of rationality and smartness. We are gut thinkers first and rational agents second, caring more about where we belong than what the latest statistics have to tell us. Politicians and educators need to remember that the intelligence of feeling needs as much if not more lesson time than sums and spelling tests.

Intelligent genes

It has been difficult to give a reasonable definition of intelligence without courting controversy. Assumptions of intellectual, racial and cultural superiority prevailed as 'advanced' nations began to colonise what they perceived to be 'backward' peoples. They blanked evidence that Africans had once built great cities, Polynesians had navigated vast expanses of ocean without a compass, and the Chinese had already invented clocks, gunpowder and printing before these things were 'discovered' in Europe.

In the nineteenth century this hierarchical logic was applied to class as well as race. The poor carry inferior or 'bad' genes, and breed more profusely, so it is inevitable that more will die of starvation. The 'science' of eugenics favoured the removal of chronically debauched undesirables from the gene pool, to allow vigorous and energetic 'good stock' to flourish. Such thinking reached its nadir in the gas chambers of Auschwitz, but it is unfair to single out Nazi ideology for blame. Eugenic ideas were also popular in Britain, France and America.

Alfred Binet instituted the idea of intelligence tests around 1900 in France. His intention was to identify those who needed help, but within a generation Lewis Terman in the USA was developing one-off tests to single out idiots, morons and imbeciles. There was little understanding of growth, change, or the moment of inspiration that ignites a dormant passion.

Not only was intelligence glibly assumed to be measurable and reducible to a single digit, it was heritable, and therefore fixed for life. Some, usually white males belonging to the wealthy middle classes, had lots of it. Most, including natives, working class people and women, did not.

Alfred Binet

1857–1911

Binet came up with the idea of the intelligence test, but his motivation was to identify those who needed help, not those who had already won the genetic lottery.

Psychologists spent thousands of hours measuring anything that was measurable, such as skull size, memory, reaction times, vocabulary and attention span. Biologists hunted for the chromosomes responsible for intelligence, and pairs of identical twins were singled out for endless studies to prove that IQ is genetic, laying the foundation for a simple formula: clever parents produce clever children.

It took decades for the truth to dawn. Genes are suspended in a complex molecular soup, and the flavour we get is affected by what else is on the menu. It is hardly surprising that the children of motivated parents with powerful social connections and deep purses tend to do better in school than children born into poverty. Adopted children at first perform to the potential of their birth parents, but respond increasingly to the influence and encouragement of their adoptive parents as the years pass.

The study of epigenetics shows that genes do not have one-on-one outcomes, but work in complex combinations, triggered by circumstances. Twin studies don't *always* show that 'the genes do the talking'. Sometimes one twin can succumb to depression or obesity while the other does not, suggesting that genes can express themselves differently in individual minds and bodies.

Intelligence is about fifty per cent heritable, which is the work of nature. That leaves a lot of scope for opportunity, aspiration and expectation, which is the work of nurture. The Flynn Effect shows that immigrants usually score poorly in intelligence tests on arrival in a new country, but by the second or third generation some of their children are applying to be doctors and teachers.

After the horrors of the Holocaust eugenics remains a taboo subject, though it has been revived in 'associative assorting' studies of clusters of people with similar genetic histories. Tiny genetic differences across populations seem to correlate with overall academic performance.

Being given a prognosis based on genetic probabilities does not however particularly help parents faced with bewildering choices for their children's education: early cramming, learning by discovery, tiger parenting, private tuition, home schooling, hothousing, academic selection, single sex, streaming by ability. The essential issue is how to ensure the best future for each child without closing off possibilities too early.

An obvious answer seems to be meritocracy: give all children equal chances to prosper. This fair-sounding ideal can however lead quickly to unfair outcomes. By rewarding the brightest in the first generation, it perpetuates a cycle of unfair advantage in the second. Clever parents expect the best for their children, and are usually best placed to get it.

Intelligent tests

Perhaps IQ tests are the answer. There is a strong correlation between academic achievement, success in life and overall happiness, but this is not surprising given that IQ tests cement the bond between formal reasoning and structured schooling, leaving other types of intelligence unexplored. Intelligence becomes defined as that which is measured in IQ tests.

There are other challenges. Neural pruning in the first years of life means that children do not arrive at school with equal servings of potential just waiting to be realised. Those whose language and number skills have been less developed at home will inevitably perform less well on pencil and paper tests.

Also, early testing runs the risk of overlooking late developers whose grey 'processing' matter is still being converted by experience and learning to more densely connected white 'reasoning' matter well up to the age of thirteen. If selection is made early, they miss out.

Another challenge is that, to create culture-fair tests, they have to be standardised, which potentially favours Western, male and convergent thinking, squeezing out traditional, female and divergent responses.

A more subtle understanding of the nexus between intelligence and attainment has encouraged some governments to provide catch-up programmes for children from disadvantaged areas, and extra provision for those with special educational needs. To balance this, there have also been initiatives to enrich the experiences of gifted and talented children.

All children benefit from challenge and bright children tend to do well anyway, as the system is already designed for them. Life pigeon-holes children soon enough, without their being told from the get-go whether they have received a gold star today or they need to attend the catch-up class. It is not praise they need, which can make them complacent or afraid of being seen to fail. A better motivator at all levels of ability is recognition of effort. When shown how to do better at a task, children tend to stick at it much longer.

There has also been wider recognition that brains are diverse and intelligence is multiple, crossing all domains and contributing widely to human flourishing. There is intelligence of the body, which earns some sports stars large sums of money. There are emotional, spiritual, artistic and moral intelligences, which cannot be measured but are equally essential to rounded personal development and the wellbeing of society.

Aristotle equated intelligence with virtue, or making wise life-choices. As usual, he was on to something important. We all know people who are bright but have made very little of their lives, and others who have made much of modest beginnings. Qualities such as attention, passion, vision, persistence and motivation are much better indicators of what we might make of ourselves, or how happy our life might be.

Having a good memory, extensive vocabulary and quick intellect is not by itself enough to be top of the form, though these gifts open many doors. Studies show that working memory, or being able to hold several things in mind at once and see them through to a conclusion, is an important determinant of future success.

It also helps to be able to look both ways at once, and to hold contrasting ideas in mind simultaneously.

What matters most is choosing the right strategy for the job at hand. Multitasking makes us versatile, but it can also dilute our concentration. We also need to know when and how to shut off all distractions so that we can give something our full attention.

Education has to keep pace with the changing demands of a 'knowledge economy'. Tests show a decline in our ability to retain knowledge as facts, but an increase in reasoning skills. Given that life requires ever more flexible responses from us, not just an ability to list what we know, smartness has to include our capacity to keep on adjusting to new learning styles in a rapidly moving digital world. Most crucially we need the ability to change tack when we realise we have taken the wrong option.

Some accuse modern education of making a generation of 'snowflakes' who can't cope with setback or failure. A day spent in the corridors of a busy school in a tough neighbourhood soon puts this fantasy to flight. We can't all win the glittering prizes or be brain surgeons. This is just as well, because society doesn't need lots of brain surgeons. It needs people who sweep our streets and empty our bins, and who are respected for doing so.

Each generation deserves a genuine chance to flourish, regardless of gender, colour and social background. Wasted potential is the real failure. If we win the genetic lottery and are given a clear run at climbing to the top of the ladder, we should be humbly thankful, and make it our business to pay something back.

Sheer genius

Visionaries and eccentrics have driven evolution forward, but genius of any kind is extremely rare, as likely to pop up in the home of a farm labourer as a palace. It demands extraordinary neural wiring, which may be an accident, and intense dedication, which is an effort of the will.

It's not enough to be born a genius. A field of knowledge has to be mastered, interrogated by questions that no one has asked before, and answered with insights we didn't know were there to be had. Courage is needed too. It's dangerous challenging orthodoxy, as many heretics have discovered, and there is always the risk of being wrong. Einstein was wrong on several things, but crucially right when it mattered. Thomas Alva Edison remarked that he couldn't have succeeded without the ten thousand failures along the way.

Perhaps it was a lone genius who saw how a contraption for squeezing the juice out of grapes could be combined with moveable type to make a printing press. Nowadays intellectual breakthroughs tend to come from groups of minds who collaborate, network their knowledge, challenge each other and rely on their diversity to make unusual connections across domains.

We can't all be geniuses, nor can we make ourselves cleverer, except by taking thought about our understanding of things. Brain implants won't up our IQ, nor will drugs except at the expense of other brain functions, though there is evidence that certain activities such as learning to play a musical instrument can reconfigure our prefrontal cortex.

Given opportunity, encouragement and grit we can become the person we have it within ourselves to be. We may not shine in all areas but we can become better at each thing we do. Original ideas are given to very few but we can be creative, if by that we mean combining what we already know to arrive at a synthesis that is new *for us*. Genius favours the prepared mind, but breakthroughs can come in moments of idleness and quiet reflection, not while we are actively striving after them.

Aristotle called us the rational animal, not because we can be clever but because we can learn how to keep things in proportion. We do not fulfil ourselves as human beings until we show that we can balance our thinking with our feeling. That's what makes us truly smart.

7 What unites us?

Theory of mind, empathy, reciprocity, compassion, altruism, aggression, non-zero sum games, tolerance, pluralism and neurodiversity.

I am a man, and I consider nothing human alien to me. *Terence, Roman playwright*

> *There is more that unites us than divides us.*

Reading other minds

Hermits elect to live alone, but that's not our natural state. We are born into the arms of a mother and raised within a nurturing family. Whether we later choose to tighten or loosen our social bonds or live together or separately, we cannot escape the madding crowd. Whatever our politics, solidarity is a better long-term policy than isolationism.

To help us in our game of social and political chess, we have inherited a cognitive skill called theory of mind. Our evolution as a social species has moulded our thought and feeling in equal measure. When we think socially, we think differently, and in many ways better. When we talk to a real person, our empathy circuit fires more strongly than when we speak remotely, or play a computer game.

Theory of mind starts with the eyes, which serve as the windows of the soul. Chimpanzees spend a lot of time looking at each other but we take it to a new level. Their eyes are dark but we have white sclera, which means we can track direction of gaze very sensitively. We know when someone has eyes only for us and we hate being stared at. Without moving our body we can point with our eyes, a mere glance giving away someone's hiding place.

We also read meaning and intention into each other's actions. If we see someone standing with arms full of shopping in front of a closed door, our instinct is to open it for them, because theory of mind is a hall of mirrors where I can see into your mind even as you see into mine.

A baby learns these mind-reading skills very early. She seeks out her mother's face immediately after birth, staring long into her eyes, establishing her first I/you dyad. She can't see her own face, but she can see herself recognised in the face of her mother. To look is to see, and to be seen is to exist. If mother smiles or sticks out her tongue, she reciprocates the gesture. If mother rolls a ball to her, she's certain to return it, as if preparing herself for the give-and-take of conversation. Gradually she learns that other people, like her, are free agents with purposes of their own.

But she also learns the dark arts of deceit, well taught by siblings and peers. At first she is the patsy in their games, but gradually she realises that she too can keep secrets. She hides her sweets when she thinks they are not looking. Even crows are careful about hiding their food finds from each other, and young male chimps make sure the alpha male isn't looking when they flirt with the females.

We are primates too, constantly acting a part, rehearsing strategies of persuasion and manipulation. Our childhood 'fibbing' is not dishonesty but essential preparation for what lies ahead. As time passes we learn from friends, fiction, film and social media not just how to read the human heart, but more importantly how to defend ourselves against the sleights that others will almost certainly practise upon us. They also teach us how to care and share, a moral urge that chimps feel only in rudimentary form, though bonobos seem more attuned to each other's needs.

Sharing is not automatic in the realpolitik of the world where we encounter extraordinary levels of deception, involving false briefings, half-truths, bluffs, counterespionage, double dealing, brazen lies and the calculated keeping of secrets. We don't particularly object to this because we're just as guilty of hypocrisy, even if well meant. When a friend asks whether she looks good in that dress, especially if she is recovering from illness, we're not likely to tell her the truth.

This is tact at work, neither harmful nor treacherous. Ambition however calls for sterner stuff. The Renaissance thinker Niccolò Machiavelli advised us that, if we want to get to the top and stay there, we should watch our back, suspect everyone, trust our enemies little and our friends even less. Ruthlessness and deception take us further than popularity and plain speaking.

Machiavellianism is not however a sustainable strategy. If everyone lied all the time, promises and pledges would become meaningless and truth would lose its currency. If everyone hid behind a false face or kept secrets, reputation, loyalty and honesty would become charades. In the end it comes down to trust, which has to be earned. When we go shopping, we return to the stores where we were told the truth and given good after-service. We judge each other by our actions, not our words.

Feeling empathy

Given the wiles of the world, how can we ever find it within ourselves to be kind to each other? The answer lies in a close connection in our brain between our theory of mind and our empathy circuit. The 'cuddle chemical' oxytocin bonds mother and child together after birth, causing even the father's heart to melt. Empathy is nature's way of getting families to stay together long enough to nurture a vulnerable new life in the human community.

This circle of support includes close kin, who can provide wider protection. Children denied secure attachment in their early years experience poor emotional bonding, potentially leading to an empathy deficit in later years. They may become the ones best placed to follow Machiavelli's advice, not letting their conscience get in the way of their ambitions.

Empathy is between-ness, achieved through our ability to feel in and through others. We get a shot of it when we hear someone laugh and experience a pang when we see someone in pain. In our brain, mirror neurons fire in sympathy. We can suppress these signals, quickening our pace past the homeless person in the doorway, blanking the fact that, in another life, that person might be us. There is something of the psychopath in all of us, recognising a feeling but quickly deadening it if it is inconvenient.

What obligation is there to care for a complete stranger anyway? Some biologists have tried to correlate the strength of our altruism with the number of genes we share with others. We're more likely to dive into a raging torrent to save our daughter than a random swimmer in difficulties.

Such a cold calculation did not occur to the Good Samaritan, who refused to pass by on the other side. Coming across the victim of a robbery on the road, he saw him as a person in need, not a batch of unrelated DNA. He bandaged his wounds, took him to the next town and paid for his medical care. This is radical empathy at work, the impulse to care for a total stranger, even to love the sinner, while expecting nothing in return.

It is not all good news with oxytocin. It can unite the clan against the out-group, creating an 'us and them' mentality. Harsh conditions on the African savannah held us in a moral bind. We needed to share, but we also needed to protect our own. Altruism was evolution's response to the first impulse, aggression towards outsiders the second. Tribal thinking, standing armies and nuclear arsenals are the legacies of this uneasy tension.

Theory of mind, oxytocin and empathy leave us with a paradoxical human nature. We can be by turns saviours or killers, saints or brutes, benefactors or avengers. We can sympathise with another's suffering or exploit it to our own advantage. We can be fiercely loyal to our own team but treat the opposition as subhuman. Depending on what is to be gained or lost, we can practise mutual aid or opt for naked self interest.

Killer gorillas

So are we a naturally aggressive species, a psychotic ape that only pretends to love peace and goodwill? It depends where we look and how we read the evidence. In the Balkans in the 1990s ancient enmities erupted into genocide between communities who had been living together peacefully for centuries, at least on the surface.

In the Amazon, Yanomamo tribesmen are often held up as the epitome of male aggression, but they turn out to be as capable as their neighbours of living peaceably together. What triggers their disputes is scarcity of resources in their challenging environment. In other tribes violence is almost unheard of, unless introduced from outside. The Piraha have no word for murder, and if it does happen, the offender is quickly ostracised or eliminated to protect the community from pollution and corruption.

History shows that when violence does erupt, goodness can be triggered as well as evil. In the appalling terrorist attacks of recent years, the viciousness of the perpetrators, who are few in number, is dwarfed by the humanity and compassion of the survivors, comforting each other even as they lie dying. In zones of bitter conflict after years of bloodletting, truth and reconciliation commissions have enjoyed some success in breaking the cycle of revenge killings.

In the 1960s there was a fashion for portraying our species as the Killer Ape. Fossil finds of smashed skulls and bodies skewered by arrow heads suggested that there had been violence in Eden. The seeds for the Killing Fields of Cambodia were sown here.

THE STUPENDOUS STORY OF US

So how bloody was life on the savannah? The distant past exists only in our imagination, but we can assume that, alongside long spells of peace and cooperation, there were also occasional skirmishes between clans of hunter gatherers, mainly over territory, resources and access to females. As late as the 1950s, New Guinea tribes were inflicting serious damage on each other. Young warriors were brought up *expecting* to kill in battle, and casualties were high in proportion to the total population.

In these tribal skirmishes, arrows could kill from a distance, hand weapons were deadly in close combat and injuries were usually fatal, but the death toll was sustainable because there was a balance of power, both sides being equally poorly armed. The huge armies of massed ranks sent out with swords and scimitars to subjugate vassal states by rape and pillage came much later.

The puzzle for anthropologists and moralists is that clans fought people they regularly exchanged goods and marriage partners with, and who spoke the same language as them, so a more primitive impulse than cultural difference was at work. When religion became organised, it divided people further. The commandment 'Thou shalt not kill' extended only to co-religionists, not heathens or infidels.

The flip side to this maladaptive trait of organised violence is that skeletons have been found with healed bones, suggesting that the sick and injured were looked after. Life was hard, but it wasn't necessarily brutal. In order for us to be here today, our ancestors must have been more prosocial than antisocial.

Linguists point to the high number of words for shame in all languages as evidence of a deep-rooted commitment to the collective cause. Geneticists point out that, despite all our differences, Homo sapiens is a single species, so our forebears must have enjoyed more fraternising than fratricide.

The modern world is still plagued by wars but they tend to be limited in scope, and always in somebody else's back yard. It seems counterintuitive, but we stand far less chance of being killed as a result of internecine strife than at any time in our history. Honour-killings and vendettas survive in some traditions, but they are rarities. Murder rates have plummeted across the world since records began, the dark deed usually inflicted on those known to the perpetrator, not randomly on strangers.

The death toll from raids and vendettas fell significantly once states grew large enough to pass laws which enabled grudges to be settled without bloodshed. The takeaway here is that war diminishes when the urges that inflame it are controlled, flashpoints are avoided and the rule of law flourishes.

Some anthropologists suggest that empathy and altruism were forged in the crucible of the human family and shared parenting. Up to a quarter of deaths among gorillas are brought about by rampaging males, which have evolved to be twice the size of females in order to protect their harem. It is not uncommon for them to kill young gorillas sired by rivals in order to bring the females into oestrus.

The breakthrough in human culture seems to have been the adoption of monogamy. As men became convinced of their paternity with a single partner, there was no longer any need for the bloody locking of horns with rivals, rape or infanticide. Men could become fathers engaged in the care and tending of their children, in it for the long term.

Not before time, say modern mothers. Babies are emotionally demanding, energy-hungry and take a long time to mature. Chimpanzee mothers are generally burdened with guarding their young from rival males and jealous females, but human mothers require the support of fathers, the protection of the extended family and the sharing of resources beyond immediate kin. Such cooperation and mutuality opened the door to full humanity, preceding the big brain, language and toolmaking by up to a million years.

Taming ourselves

It seems we have modelled ourselves on peace-loving bonobos, not ill-tempered gorillas. Our ancestors knew from the domestication of wild oxen that selecting more docile bulls could create more manageable beasts of burden. By turning this logic on our own kind we have slowly bred aggression, violence and warmongering out of ourselves.

If a chieftain grabbed power by violent means and threatened to kill upstarts, the more peaceable males in the clan soon worked out that, working as a coalition, they were stronger than him. Murdering the tyrant not only made life more tolerable for everyone, it removed his genes from the gene pool.

Through a strange process called neoteny, we have 'bred' ourselves to stay young, reducing testosterone-fuelled thuggery dramatically. With our short snout and round face we remain hairless, playful and, crucially, low on the aggression scale. Without this last assurance, we could not walk alone through the dark streets of an unfamiliar neighbourhood in a city of millions of strangers and expect to get home safely.

The law proscribes murder but leaves the door open to judicial execution, self defence and killing in the name of 'just war', exemplified in the code of chivalry. An alpha male wolf ceases to be aggressive when its rival rolls over and exposes its soft underbelly, a gesture of submission which flicks an 'off' switch in the aggressor's brain. The problem for modern wagers of war is that their drones and missiles can't detect such signals, so there is no way of turning down the aggression dial.

Peacemaking, courtliness and the banning of arbitrary punishments also helped to encourage civility, replacing the vicious cycle of conquest and oppression with a virtuous one of co-existence and moderation. Our modern standoff of hawks and doves, with equal numbers of wall-erectors and bridge-builders on either side, is the precarious legacy of lessons only half-learned on the savannah.

This playbook was written too late for Genghis Khan, who impregnated hundreds of women along the route of his conquests, with or without their consent. Military clout and physical strength are not however the same as the urge to rape, or having a high sex drive. Not all leaders or weightlifters are macho thugs, or leave a trail of orphans behind them.

It is a moot point whether Genghis was taking advantage of his status as a red-blooded male, behaving boorishly or in thrall to his selfish genes. Either way, DNA studies suggest that an estimated sixteen million people carry a little bit of Genghis inside them.

We cannot however pin the blame for bad behaviour of any kind on testosterone or our genes. We have priorities other than filling the world with smaller versions of ourselves, and in any case the same genes are involved in urging us to look after ourselves one day and reach out to each other the next. *We* decide our response, not our genes or sex hormones.

Nor need we demonise anger and aggression. They are essential ingredients in our emotional repertoire, necessary when we feel we can no longer stay silent, which is not the same as licensing violence. Righteous indignation is justified when a great wrong has been done, and wrathful compassion is appropriate when loved ones or friends need to be saved from their own vices.

We take such action because caring comes as naturally to us as looking out for our own. This does not make hypocritical egoists of us all. 'I care for you because

I want to be cared for in return' is a sensible deal for individuals who realise they need each other to survive.

Widening our moral circle

So can we claim to be natural altruists? In the animal kingdom we see the immense sacrifices parents make for their offspring, or in the case of social insects, for their colony. These responses tend to be made however in response to specific cues. The mother wren cannot *not* risk her life in the face of a threat to her chicks. There are even cases of lions rearing antelope, not because they 'love' them, but because their parenting instinct is so strong.

Human altruism is different, involving the promotion of the welfare of others, even when there is a cost to ourselves. We have evolved as natural co-operators, not selfish loners. As we saw with the Good Samaritan, and we see today with life-boat crews, open-hearted generosity can extend to complete strangers who share none of our genes. Empathy-driven ethical behaviour might have started out as thinly disguised self-interest, but as our frontal lobes developed it matured into selfless compassion, on the principle that 'I cannot be happy if I see you suffering alongside me'.

We can give without expecting anything in return. Some donate blood or a bodily organ, not knowing who will receive them. The cynic might still insist that this is self-interest at work, but he also hopes that, when he is hospitalised in a strange town, the organisers of the local blood bank aren't all cynics. He might note too that, where cash is offered for blood, less is collected. Altruism, it seems, is not for sale.

Our ancestors were not pushovers when it came to fairness and the rule of law. Strong reciprocity works because it has teeth: those who break the bond of trust, such as cheats and free-riders, face punishment. As we find out when we upset our neighbours or break the law, society's norms are constantly enforced by violation-spotters, whether they are local nosey-parkers or remote tax inspectors. We have a reputation to keep, and if we don't manage it carefully, we might find ourselves cut dead in the street, sent to prison or banished from the community.

As part of the deal we cut with society we uphold the ideals of justice and mercy, not because we are holier-than-thou, but because one day we might be in need of them. Recognising our individual weakness is a source of collective strength. This was not the view of the philosopher Friedrich Nietzsche, who hated the idea of the weak ganging up against the strong. The world belongs not to the meek of heart but to the noble of soul who show us how to rise to the top, and stay there.

Two seventeenth century English thinkers offer us contrasting solutions to Nietzsche's challenge. Thomas Hobbes, who lived through the bloodshed of the Civil War, believed we are selfish and aggressive creatures, trapped in a dog-eat-dog existence. Only firm government and strong policing can protect us from each other.

Writing a generation later, after peace had been restored, John Locke proposed the notion of a social pact. As long as we accept our differences and do nothing to harm each other, we can agree to live together amicably. If we don't, we find ourselves engaged in endless zero-sum games, or lose/lose confrontations.

John Locke

1632–1704

Having survived the bloodbath of the English Civil War, Locke pleaded for toleration and the separation of religion and politics. It's better to strike a deal. His ideas inspired the American Declaration of Independence, but zero-sum games still abound.

If I damage your car by accident, and the next day you come and break my window to settle the score, neither of us wins. If I pay my taxes and you don't, you win and I lose, which is neither fair nor sustainable. As Charles Darwin noted, a society of swindlers, thieves and freeloaders would not hold out long against one which cooperated and pooled resources. More terminally, if evolution had played out as a zero sum game in which all the little fish get eaten by the big fish, all life would go extinct because the ocean would soon be empty.

Winning games

What we need to play is a non-zero sum game in which everyone gets something without losing too much. This ethic guides the choices of every cell in our body.

We are healthy when our heart cells play on the same team as our liver cells. Cancer cells are so deadly because they are out only for themselves, multiplying uncontrollably, sabotaging the commonwealth. Mutual aid is the best policy.

This principle applies equally to the 'invisible hand' of the global economy. If we trade with each other, we each get a little richer. Protectionism shuts us both out. Not all trade deals are fair, but no-one knowingly chooses to be a loser. If I start ahead of you, it's in my interest to help you catch up, because then you can afford to buy more of my products.

In the wider social sphere we have to learn to live with difference, which calls for toleration. If you insist that greed is good and I think it is bad, we have to find a way of meeting in the middle so that we both get something out of the deal. On matters of opinion, we can both be right to the extent that we can justify our argument. On matters of fact, we are not free to invent the facts to fit our theory.

This is particularly problematic when it comes to religious beliefs, where gods are given different names and institute different commandments. They can't all be right. Toleration is all very well, but what happens when we feel we are confronted with the intolerable?

John Locke's solution was to separate the secular from the religious realm. We should be free to hold any private beliefs we wish to, so long as we publicly obey the laws of the land and do not try to force our beliefs down other people's throats. It may well transpire that we are wrong and they were right all along.

By and large this model of mutual tolerance works well, breaking down only when we feel that the liberties of others are being threatened, in which case we have to intervene. We no longer go to war for religious reasons, but extremists and fundamentalists make consensus and co-existence difficult if not impossible. Given that our journey through life obliges us to choose an ideology or overarching story to guide us on our way, we might as well commit to one that is life-affirming and other-regarding, not rooted in fear and mistrust.

We are bound to see things from different points of view because we are all born into particular situations and guilty of motivated reasoning. We don't coolly study the facts and then adopt a cause. We feel a passion, then find the data to support it, regardless of how 'educated' we are, or how 'rational' we feel. It's not so much a matter of what we *want* to believe, more what we feel we *must* believe.

Opinions are easy to come by, but thinking critically is hard. Given our capacity to be plain mistaken, get the wrong end of the stick and turn our errors into grievances, it pays to keep an open mind, be aware of the designs that others have on our beliefs, and submit our thoughts to a regular detox.

We should not deny others the right to think differently, nor should we disseminate facts that bear no relation to the actual state of the world. Reasoned debate leaves both of us free to argue another day, but total commitment to a cause risks a zero-sum game of mutual destruction.

History shows how quick we have been to ostracise those who don't fit into our moral frame: lepers, savages, heretics, gypsies, lunatics, the disabled, witches, homosexuals. The degree to which we accept such groups into the human family is a fair measure of our claim to consider ourselves civilised.

The term 'neurodiverse' has entered our vocabulary in recent years to give a new gloss to an ancient truth: we need a pluralistic approach to human affairs, because each mind is differently moulded. Brain scans give us fresh understanding of conditions and illnesses which previously left their sufferers abandoned outside the city gates, perhaps stoned to death for being mad, bad, or a threat to the body politic. Nowadays we have given demonic possession new names: epilepsy, schizophrenia, bipolar, Tourette's and multiple personality disorder.

Unlike conspiracy theorists, people with these conditions have not chosen to be this way. They are not cursed, morally depraved or a danger to the rest of us. They need our understanding, not our disdain. Theory of mind, empathy, compassion, toleration, pluralism, critical thinking and neurodiversity converge to confirm a core truth, put to the test every time we venture beyond our front door: there are more things that unite us than divide us.

8 What divides us?

Gender bias, racism, inequality, class prejudice, indoctrination, nationalism, culture wars, failure to find common ground.

All animals are equal, but some animals are more equal than others. *George Orwell*

> *In our differences lie our strengths, not our weaknesses.*

Gender and sexism

A quick glance at the natural world reveals that variety is the norm, orchestrated by sex, which is nature's way of creating novelty out of difference. No two organisms are physically the same. It cannot be otherwise. How then do natural differences of sex become embroiled in divisive wars about gender?

The answer is that, while sexual determination is biological, gender identity is cultural. The physical differentiation starts straightforwardly enough around six weeks after conception, when our body starts to grow the sexual organs of a girl or a boy, and our brain is sexed by powerful hormones. Embryonic girls retain XX on their twenty-third chromosome while little boys become XY.

In other words females are the first sex, not males, maleness not arriving on the scene until life was already a billion years old. Biologists are still puzzling out whether evolution 'invented' males to create genetic variety that cloning could not alone provide. After the delivery of a tiny sperm cell the job of the male is done, a small service that can now be performed by artificial insemination by donor or in vitro.

However initiated, the sexing of the body and mind do not always follow a binary pattern. Gender dysphoria occurs when the psychological awareness of gender no longer matches the biological sex of the body. The little boy feels deep inside that he is 'really' a girl, and the little girl does not want to grow breasts or have periods.

If this feeling persists, it calls for sensitive counselling, followed possibly by life-changing hormone treatment and surgery. For this to happen, society must be prepared to redefine what a man or a woman 'essentially' is. This is challenging if we feel there is no room for plurality along a continuum that can accommodate those who do not conform to sexual norms. Some believe that genetic destiny is absolute, sexual orientation is immutable, gender cannot be changed, and any deviation from what they approve is anathema.

Homosexuality is common in nature, but condemnation of gays is powerful among those who believe that anything outside heterosexual sex is an abomination. Others insist that trans people should be classified solely on whether they possess a penis or vagina, with nothing in between. This dogma does not help those born with ambiguous sexual organs, who already struggle to integrate their sexuality with social expectation. At the very least, they need to feel free to choose which public toilet they use.

The battle of the sexes

Despite these moral complexities our species opted for sexual reproduction, not cloning, because mixing genes makes stronger organisms, mitigates chemical damage, outwits predators and makes us smarter, though it also makes us live fast and die young, in relative terms.

In some cases, such as the female spider devouring the male straight after copulation, mating can look like a deadly battle of the sexes, which makes our gender wars look tame by comparison. Eating our partner after sex could hardly work for highly social animals like ourselves, whose offspring need lengthy post-natal care from both parents, supported by a whole community.

Anthropologists believe that on the savannah women were as strong and resourceful as men, foraging at least as many calories for the tribe, if not more. For many millennia, men did not understand their role in planting the seed. Every mammal on earth starts life in a mother's womb, but the making of new life was a great mystery, resulting in women not just enjoying equal status but being revered as goddesses of fertility and fecundity. This does not mean there was free love. The monogamous pair bond prevailed, helping the family to evolve as a stable unit for all its members.

So why were friendly female earth spirits ousted by angry male sky gods? Why did matriarchy morph into patriarchy? Why were the male of the species routinely taught to see women as defective men? Why did women come to be screened behind veils, hidden away while menstruating, clamped with chastity belts, demonised as sexual predators, burned as witches, treated as chattels and shackled to chaperones? Why, in the twenty-first century, is misogyny so endemic that some want it to be treated as a hate crime?

There are several reasons. As our ancestors moved into permanent settlements, males began to accumulate livestock, acreage and property. Gradually women too became viewed as economic goods. Trading them between neighbouring clans helped to cement political alliances.

Sexual politics played their part too. Once men discovered their role in inseminating a woman, they became obsessed with paternity rights. Women became valuable baby-making machines, their fidelity a guarantee of property passed on through the male line. Sexual jealousy became a powerful sociopolitical force, as the story of Helen of Troy shows.

Religion played its part too. The myth of Eve stealing the apple in the Garden of Eden created a culture of women as venal temptresses, barely rational and certainly not to be trusted. The cult of the Virgin Mary corrected the balance to a degree, but both myths painted women into a corner. For generations they had a choice of being a prostitute, a nun or a compliant wife. The one role they couldn't assume was a self-supporting independent spirit who was the equal of any man.

All of these prehistoric 'just so' stories feed into the systemic sexism which still condemns women to lower pay and fewer top jobs, not to mention wife beating, female genital mutilation, femicide and constant subjection to the 'male gaze'. In some countries, millions of baby girls are 'missing', aborted or killed at birth because they have no economic value. Women worldwide still have to fight hard to get their due, assert ownership of their body and challenge stringent abortion laws passed by male-dominated legislatures.

Feminists have made many gains, debunking stereotypes of strong, hard, cold and dry men lording it over weak, soft, warm and moist women. They cannot agree however whether women, other than in the fact that they menstruate, are quintessentially different from men, seeing and experiencing the world differently. When we read a novel, do we know instinctively the sex of the author? Do we prefer a male doctor, or would we rather be sentenced by a female judge?

Radical feminists insist that a woman can do whatever a man can do, just as well if not better, especially when it comes to giving birth. They see the biology of the body as incidental, even though children as young as three have worked out what little boys and girls are made of. These expectations, they say, are socially constructed 'performances', or expectations that men inflict on women, because it suits them.

Across the world, men still have a long way to go in shaking off the prejudices of the past. Many struggle to cope with social changes that they feel threaten their masculinity. Many women still don't feel safe or treated equitably. If relationships between the sexes are to flourish, boys need to be brought up to respect girls, and sheltered from dehumanising pornography which 'sells' sex as abuse of women, not mutual pleasure.

Race and racism

Race and skin colour raise as many fundamental divisions as sex and gender. Slavery was the norm in the ancient world, usually inflicted on conquered peoples who were automatically seen as inferior, whatever their complexion. It fell to Stoic philosophers, some of whom who had once been slaves, to promote the idea that a slave is also a man and a brother.

Their declaration that we are all 'racial' equals is based on sound genetic theory. Skin colour is accidental, an adaptation to the local climatic conditions of wherever our ancestors finally settled after various migrations from Africa sixty thousand years ago.

Four hundred years ago, Sir Thomas Browne remarked 'There is all Africa and her prodigies in us', intuiting the later discovery that we all share DNA with invaders from one point of the compass or another. In fact, there is a wider variety of genes between the residents of our local street than between the inhabitants of Africa and Europe.

Our subsequent history has not however honoured our common human inheritance. Empires have been founded on the notion that the colonised are ripe for economic exploitation, weaker specimens who have forfeited their rights as human beings, not descendants of Adam and Eve, and therefore not real 'people' at all. Centuries of the forced transport of millions of slaves across oceans, post-colonial immigration, refugee crises, supremacist ideology and fear of white 'replacement' by miscegenation leave modern societies struggling to create harmonious genetic and cultural melting pots.

Nearly all European nations took a bite out of the developing continents around them, usually for expansionist motives. Colonialism has left a bitter legacy of stolen lands, genocide, pillaged resources and robbed treasures. The audit of what was taken away and what was given in return is painful and controversial. Some campaign for the restitution of plundered wealth, others for the tearing down of statues and the renaming of buildings bearing the titles of those who made fortunes from the exploitation of indigenous peoples.

Pluralism and multiculturalism are far preferable to segregation, but they impose colonisation in reverse, and the need for integration. Immigrants of all colours and cultures bring new ideas and energy, often in flight from poverty or oppression, working hard at jobs that need to be filled and making sacrifices for their children to succeed. They have to battle residual prejudice and structural inequalities which make it hard to break cycles of underachievement, the blame for which often goes back to inhumane slavery practices, such as the deliberate breaking up of families.

Where racism persists, it is taught and caught, not inherited. We aren't born racist, nor do we 'see' skin colour in our early years. If we are born into an ethnic minority, becoming aware of our identity through the negative reactions of our peers in the dominant culture can be a rude awakening.

White children can grow up believing that race is invisible because they never experience racist feedback. The antidote is to raise their consciousness by talking openly about skin colour, teaching the legacy of empire, discussing positive role models from other cultures and exposing pernicious myths such as Aryan supremacy. Staying silent about race leaves prejudice unspoken, therefore unchallenged.

More or less equal

The concept of equality lies at the heart of our disputes about gender, race and class, but it is an abstraction that is hard to convert into social justice. How can we treat each other equally when we are all physically chalk and cheese?

From the moment of conception, we share a basic biological equality, in the sense that we qualify as human. Unless we are born disabled in some way, we grow four limbs and a head, but the physical similarities stop there. Some of us are destined to be tall and confident, others to be shy and go bald early.

Inequalities are built into both our biology and the situation we are born into, which inevitably differs between us. Early experiences are so crucial in determining the kind of brain we will have as an adult that the die of inequality might be cast very early. Preschooolers who are denied lots of talk, books, enriching experiences and good role models face neurological inequalities before they even get to school.

Marx and Engels, joint writers of The Communist Manifesto in 1848, were champions of equality, but they were not naive enough to suppose that equality can be absolute or amount to sameness. Instead they promoted the idea of each giving according to ability and receiving according to need. Their ire was directed at the inequalities generated by the class system, which were nearly always economic in nature.

Since then, equality has been more finely parsed, as outcome, opportunity and reward. Equality of outcome begins the moment we are born, because we all 'come out' of the womb with certain advantages or handicaps. We have no control over whether we are delivered into a palace or a slum, and on arrival, we might discover that we are congenitally tone deaf, or the shortest person in our class.

Missing out on the some of the finer delights of music is a pity, but being short, through no fault of our own, puts us at a disadvantage in the middle of a football crowd. We won't get as good a view of the action, even though we've paid the same price for our ticket. What we need is a seat nearer the front or a box to stand on, which would quite literally level the playing field for us.

This kind of fairness, as equality of opportunity, is difficult to apply evenly across the social spectrum. It's no good being the brainiest person on the block if we live in a deprived area, are sent to an underachieving school and are denied a university place because our face doesn't fit.

The principle of equity asserts that these injustices need to be addressed, which does not amount to treating everyone the same. Children given a poor start to life, perhaps because of abuse or chronic illness, need and deserve remedial care and compensatory education, without which they will never gain ground on their more fortunate peers. It won't suffice to give every parent an educational grant regardless of need, because the non-needy are already ahead of the game. In such cases, treating everyone the same is anything but fair.

Two American philosophers approach this debate about whether and how to redistribute wealth from opposite poles. John Rawls suggests a policy of 'justice as fairness': we should imagine an 'original position' in which we don't know whether we will be born a prince or a pauper. It makes sense therefore to espouse policies that ensure a fair deal for everyone.

Robert Nozick disagrees. If we are born into wealth, no-one has a right to take it from us via punitive taxes. It has been lawfully accumulated by our forebears, and now it belongs to us. Taxing the rich to give a leg-up to the poor merely replaces one form of injustice with another, and making us all equally poor discourages enterprise and responsibility.

Some anthropologists believe that if the wealth of the few had been constantly squandered on the many during our early evolution, the arts of civilisation could not have flourished. Without elite citizens who worked their way to the top by ability and effort, we would still be roaming the savannah.

Idealistic appeals to those with ability to be generous towards those in need founder on the jagged rocks of reality: not all of the poor deserve a leg-up, and the rich are not obliged to share their wealth. Equality is a pipe dream, and if the meek are destined to inherit the earth, it won't be this side of the grave. The world belongs to those who make themselves more equal by dint of their enterprise and graft.

This brings us to equality of reward. Much depends on what we do with the talents we are born with. It's no good having good hand-to-eye coordination if we can't be bothered to practise our tennis, and the gift of genius is useless without a great deal of hard work.

We debate long and hard about what rewards each job 'deserves', though the final decision is usually made by market forces, not moral persuasion. We can generally live with the idea of chief executives receiving huge bonuses, because we neither want their level of stress nor crave their jet-set lifestyle. We don't mind people wealthier than us paying privately for their health care, or their children's schooling, so long as there is a decent state school and public hospital just round the corner for us.

What offends our innate sense of fairness is when we see the cake being divided up unevenly, or one group being allowed to bury their snouts in the trough. We are more likely to get angry if people doing the same work as us receive a pay rise, and we are passed over.

Class divisions

Our ancestors were largely egalitarian because they had to be. Wealth could not be accumulated because there was nowhere to keep it, and it was too much to carry. If Ugg made a big kill, he shared it with everyone in the clan, because next week he might find himself dependent on their largesse. Many cultures operated on the basis of the gift, often extravagantly given. Making a neighbouring clan feel indebted was much more future-oriented than killing them, or constantly having to defend against their attacks.

There were no lords and ladies in the Garden of Eden, but society gradually became more stratified around the time we started to settle in cities. Rather than being a jack of all trades, it made more sense to specialise, as a cobbler or scribe. It soon became clear that the scribe earned more, worked less hard and enjoyed more privileges. This generated a constant striving, the labourer intent on becoming the overseer and the slave the master.

We all want to improve our station in life, but what if class is assigned at birth, and fixed for life? Plato believed that the happy society comprises bronze workers, silver functionaries and gold leaders, each content to know their place and not challenge it, though he was probably being ironic because he also believed in excellence being rewarded.

The doctrine of a 'natural' hierarchy was picked up by Social Darwinists in the nineteenth century. They saw genetic inferiority and social inadequacy as the same thing. There was no way out of the slums, and high child mortality among the poor was inevitable. The cries of the weak for equality and fairness were merely attempts to shame the strong into giving up some of their wealth and power.

This was not the view of Darwin himself, nor does it allow for the fact that some of us are more determined to get on, possess a specific skill that we wish to perfect, or want sell our talent more dearly. Liberal politicians recognised the need for social mobility, from which grew the idea of meritocracy as a way of encouraging aspiration and allowing the deserving to get ahead.

This works fairly for the first generation, but by the second or third, a family dynasty becomes established. Privilege is perpetuated, power is monopolised and opportunity reduced for those outside the charmed circle. The rich get richer and the poor get poorer. We might be born free, but within a generation, we're in chains, victims of the class-ceiling, which is the greatest divide of all.

Research shows that societies with the biggest gap between wealth and poverty are less cohesive, and certainly less just. The triple lock at the bottom of the pile of low pay, ill health and bad schooling is hard to break. Criminologists aren't surprised to see higher crime rates in areas that are socially deprived, or during times of economic hardship. Those wrongly accused of stealing a loaf of bread and denied legal aid cannot enjoy equality before the law as long as rich financiers can afford expensive lawyers to get them off their charge of insider dealing.

Bring on the revolution

The obvious response is to stage a revolution, except that revolutions are no guarantee of a fairer or more equal society. Swift and brutal revolutions usually usher in a more scheming and ruthless regime than the one that's just lost its head on the guillotine. No sooner are the princes, lords and nobles stripped of their assets than a new elite of autocrats, carpetbaggers and oligarchs muscles its way to the top, by fair means or foul.

Our government might try to console us with the idea that 'we're all in it together': we're all classless now, the law is colour blind and women have finally achieved parity with men. Karl Marx saw through this ploy, warning of the dangers of false consciousness. We *think* we are free and equal because that's exactly what those running the show *want* us to think. They can pull the wool over our eyes because they are the gatekeepers of what we are allowed to know, or not to know.

Whether Marx was right on this point, he got one thing badly wrong. In the name of equality, he urged common ownership of the means of production, but where communism has been practised, it has failed badly. If the village common belongs to everyone, we all have a right to graze our sheep on it when we want to. By the end of the summer all the grass is gone, and our sheep will starve in the winter.

Karl Marx
1818–1883
Marx saw revolution as the final stage in solving the injustices and inequalities of the world. Unfortunately, in those countries where his ideas have been adopted, other types of tyranny have been unleashed, and false consciousness is even more prevalent than in the capitalist West.

This is known as the tragedy of the commons, where everything belongs to everybody but nobody takes responsibility for anything. Capitalists maintain that only private ownership, driven by the profit motive, guarantees that there will be a good crop of hay next year, ensuring food for all.

This view can have even more disastrous consequences than communism. Nobody can own the air we breathe, the Arctic ice caps, the tropical forests or our dwindling supply of underground fresh water. We see the results of unregulated free-for-all in the state of the world's oceans: declining fish stocks, rafts of plastic waste, scarified seabeds and steadily rising surface temperatures. Careful stewardship of our planet can work only as a hard-struck deal between private investment and public interest.

International cooperation on global issues is one of the greatest challenges ahead because it faces the obstacle of national self-interest. Marx urged workers of the world to unite, but this was his second big miscalculation. When war broke out in 1914, it was not a class war but a war of nation states. Nationalism was largely invented by nineteenth century demagogues bent on bolstering their power and extending their influence, usually by attempting to annexe the country next door.

'My country first' is not however a sustainable evolutionary or political ploy. We share dwindling resources on an increasingly crowded planet, and there are no volunteers for standing last in the queue.

It is becoming increasingly important to work together and study each other's ways. Our political and cultural traditions define us, but they need not separate us, nor do we need to stoke the fires of 'culture wars' by dismissing as 'woke' those who want the revolution to go faster. The 'sleepy' need to be confronted with truths about the past and concerns about the future that they find uncomfortable.

Our differences are not awkward tokens in a war of ideas, but real values that claim equal status and objectively oblige us to come up with solutions. We need to establish what aspirations we share and build on them, not exaggerate our differences.

Modern brain science has shown how we are all neurodivergent, with tiny biological variations that show up on our brain scans and manifest in our life as differences of gender, race, class and belief. The choice is ours whether they serve as justifications for division and inequality, or empower us to find new solutions to the problems faced by our young and inexperienced species.

9 How do we stay positive?

Anxiety, stress, depression, mental illness, trauma, therapy, resilience, happiness and laughter.

Live frugally with a contented mind. *Lucretius*

> *Peace of mind, positivity and happiness are not birthrights. We have to make them from what we have been given.*

Staying chilled

The scene is somewhere on the African savannah, fifty thousand years ago. It's been a long day, we've failed to make a kill and we are still far from camp. We know there is a lion on the prowl nearby and a storm is brewing. We are tired, on edge and getting worried.

Worry is a normal reaction that directs us to solving a particular problem, in this case getting home safely. It is less effective if it abandons us to negative thoughts. Having a panic attack is even worse, as it incapacitates our ability to respond.

We'll stop fretting and relax by the campfire tonight, because we know where the 'off' switch is. Our stress levels, having primed us to solve our temporary problem, will reset to normal. In the morning, our body will gee us up with a fresh shot of the stress hormone cortisol to send us back out to find food to feed the family.

Just as a sapling needs the steady buffeting of the wind to strengthen its stem, so a moderate dose of stress is good for us, especially when young. If we were lucky, our parents managed our stress levels to allow us to develop psychological toughness and prepare us for the next challenge.

We also needed to be given strategies for resetting to default, because chronic stress with no foreseeable end merely stresses us about being stressed. Persistent pumping of cortisol through our veins pushes our blood pressure to dangerously high levels. It can also damage the delicate process of methylation in our body which repairs our DNA, strengthens our nerves and regulates our hormones.

The fear that something dreadful *could* happen leaves us hyper-alert even though there is no threat. We suffer constant anxiety with no particular object, which means we can't get on top of it. We feel unsettled without knowing why, our joy in the present stolen by angst about the future, which just won't go away.

Its extreme forms are anxious/avoidant behaviour, when we are afraid to come out of our shell, and paranoia, where we see everything as a threat. A little bit of constructive paranoia is good however: it really *does* pay to look both ways first when crossing the road.

Although we enjoy many more creature comforts than our ancestors and face far fewer existential threats, modern life remains psychologically taxing. Perhaps there are new stressors or we deal with the old ones less well. Religion used to be our comfort, but now we cling to other transitional objects to replace our childhood teddy: our collection of retro jewellery, football supporter's scarf, or complete set of Elvis LP's.

These assurances work for many, but anxiety, depression and most recently chronic fatigue syndrome have increasingly become part of our worry landscape. Some of us feel 'soul sick', ill at ease in the world, inconsolably bored, inexplicably sad or persistently nagged by guilt.

When we try to escape the insistent demands of the twenty-first century by going away on holiday, we might be disappointed find that it's not so easy to leave our cares behind. They have followed us in our suitcase and we are still the same person on arrival.

If our destination is a less wealthy country, the locals are probably more cheerful and resilient than we are. Without our high expectations, they do not suffer status anxiety. Without our hang-ups, they are less likely to report to their doctor with depression. In fact in their culture there might not even be a word for it.

When we get back home we rejoin the queue of the 'worried well', concerned about every missed heartbeat or sleepless night. We're all generally doing better and living longer, but feeling inexplicably worse, constantly distracted, bombarded by bad news, one step behind the action and unsure of ourselves.

We miscalculate risk, panicking over a single terror attack many miles from home but not thinking twice about making a car journey to the local shops. What our brain registers is the twenty-five thousand deaths from suicide bombs every year, usually in far-off places. What it doesn't compute is the million fatalities in car accidents during the same period, commonly less than a mile from home.

Feeling down

We're bound to feel 'under the weather' occasionally and shouldn't be surprised if our positive mood is harder to sustain on an overcast day. Every moment can't be great, and we suspect that those who claim they never feel down in the dumps are not being honest with us. We accept the occasional bad hair day as a blip in our mood from which we will recover. One day however, like the poet Dante, we might find ourselves lost in the middle of a dark wood, and it will take more than a quick pick-me-up to find our own way out.

If we're really unlucky we might experience a bout of clinical depression. This is not a character flaw or failure to 'pull ourselves together', but an invisible wound that can hurt as much as a damaged limb, with pain in every fibre. It is not an affectation, but a sign of something broken inside. One in ten of us is likely to suffer from it at some point in our lifetime, with no way of knowing whether our number will be called. If we get through life without knowing what real depression feels like, we should consider ourselves blessed.

In unipolar depression we get down and stay down, but in bipolar depression we can have marked swings between euphoria and despair. Every sufferer is different, requiring carefully tailored treatment, usually a mix of talk therapy and medication. Many manage their condition from their own resources, or suffer in silence, if only because help is hard to come by.

'Mental illness' is a broader term. Nowadays we talk more openly about it than we used to, which is good, but greater familiarity can lure us into thinking that mental health problems are temporary inconveniences, like having flu. For those who suffer them, the reality is much more gruelling. The symptoms often begin in adolescence, when the mind undergoes great changes. A worrying trend with no obvious cause is that children as young as ten are increasingly exhibiting depressed and disturbed patterns of behaviour.

Diagnosing mental illness

The key challenge in recognising mental illness, and working out the best way to treat it, is the art of diagnosis. Personality disorders such as schizophrenia, autism and Tourette's syndrome can sometimes be traced to a misfiring brain circuit or the presence of certain genes, but mental breakdowns, brought on as much by nurture as nature, have no biological markers. They are much harder to diagnose and therefore much more complex to treat.

The Diagnostic Statistical Manual of Mental Disorders used by psychiatrists lists a hundred and fifty classifications, dismissed by some as scientifically meaningless. There are regular deletions and additions, sometimes dictated by cultural fashion. There seemed for instance to be an 'outbreak' of multiple personality disorder in the 1990s.

The challenge for diagnosticians is that mental illness occurs out of sight, behind and beyond obvious physical symptoms. It belongs to a whole person experiencing a bewildering flow of perceptions and memories. It happens in an embodied mind, not confined to a misbehaving brain. Only the depressed person knows the toxic mix of low self-esteem, poor concentration, restlessness and a sense of the world appearing flat and colourless.

These are moods, part of who we are, based on feelings which are too close to hold at arm's length. Normally we are able to listen to our body, but depression can make us feel a stranger in our own home, exacerbated if we feel critical towards ourselves, or angry at the world. If we become incapable of regulating our anxieties, they can manifest physically as stomach cramps, back pain, hair loss and constant fatigue, because our body keeps the score.

Trauma, whether as chronic abuse or one-off catastrophe, can cause a much deeper rift between mind and body, resulting in one dissociating from the other. The symptoms can manifest as conversion disorder, emerging some time after the event, then lasting for many years. It used to be dismissed as malingering, but it is now understood as catastrophic loss of agency and troubling separation of aspects of the self.

To shield their mind from gazing at the Gorgon some sufferers go blind, even though their visual cortex is healthy. In order to protect the 'good me', they create a 'bad me' to act as a scapegoat or whipping boy, which can lead to thoughts of self-harming. In a condition known as 'neglect' some lose control of one side of their body, even though their nervous system is intact.

Some accuse psychiatrists of mythologising mental illness to give credibility to their profession. Up to thirty types of schizophrenia have been identified, characterised by hearing voices in the head, but the number is beside the point. All that schizophrenics know is that the voices are real and tormenting.

The causes of mental illness might lie outside the brain, in an imbalance between the biology of the body, the experience of the mind and the quality of social relations, perhaps going back to insecure attachment in childhood or unresolved stress in the present.

Alternatively, the causes might reside inside the brain itself, though with a hundred billion neurons to sift through, locating them is nigh impossible. So far over forty contributory genes have been identified, but no-one knows what triggers them, how they combine, or how they change the flow of messages between synapses. We rely on our executive network to keep our sensory inputs and emotional responses in harmony but when we're depressed, we feel over-sensitive to what is going on around us, or to what others might be saying about us.

Other suspects include serotonin deficiency, too many beta waves assailing the brain, an inflamed immune system affecting brain chemistry, an overactive right brain, an enlarged fear centre in the brain, an 'at risk' personality type, or a bad experience such as abuse, divorce, redundancy and bereavement, buried deep and needing to be worked through. Sometimes, as with Hamlet, it might be a case of succumbing to the 'pale cast of thought' through over-thinking a problem. The least likely cause of mental illness, given its crippling effects, is taking it on as a lifestyle choice.

Ministering to a mind diseased

If diagnosis is difficult, treatment is even more so. The best and most lasting therapy marries the art of the soul with the science of the body, and the good therapist promotes resourceful self-help before prescribing medication as a last resort.

Some patients respond to anti-depressants which modulate serotonin re-uptake in the brain, but they don't work for all and there is disagreement whether serotonin is the principal player in the piece. In clinical trials these drugs outperform placebos, but only just.

Cognitive behaviour therapy (CBT) works for some, based on the principle that if the thoughts behind the behaviour can be changed, the feelings will follow suit. Phobias are learned, not instinctive, and with skilful desensitisation techniques can be unlearned.

CBT's drawback as a treatment is that it relies heavily on rational solutions, which can't easily convert turbulent emotions into tractable cognitions. It does not always get at the root cause, only masks it, because it takes more than six half-hour sessions to 'rewire' the brain.

Others opt for a 'talking cure' involving lengthy sessions with a trained therapist, who must have the ears of an owl, the wisdom of a sage, the imagination of a novelist, the patience of Job and a special feel for such a difficult job.

We tend to think of mental illness as an emotional affliction, but there is a strong cognitive dimension too, which is why talking about it helps. We can't reason our way out of depression, but we can use language to help us separate 'our brain' from what it is doing to 'us'. Words can distance us from our thoughts and feelings, then allow us to own them by bringing them closer. Creative writing can be a powerful form of self-discovery, helping us to understand what we think by seeing what we have to say.

Meanwhile, there is a catalogue of alternative therapies for mending a broken mind and a host of 'emotional freedom techniques' for massaging a troubled soul, from the well-researched to the far-out. These include acupuncture, reflexology, primal screaming, linguistic programming, homeopathy, eye movement desensitisation, herbalism, transcendental meditation, body tapping, crystal healing and art therapy, to name a few.

Depression in history

Even though depression doesn't seem a particularly useful evolutionary adaptation, we can assume that it has always been with us, though not by that name. Some cultures have no concept of it, but that doesn't mean that the condition does not exist, only that it has been interpreted differently.

Christianity viewed despair as a sin against the Holy Ghost. If we focus our attention on higher things, our worldly cares soon vanish. Monks were chided for the sin of sloth, or not keeping themselves busy through work. 'Low spirits' were described as melancholy, resulting from having too much black bile in the blood, or being under the spell of Saturn, the gloomy planet.

The affectation of melancholy was a luxury granted only to wealthy males who could afford to temper their sadness with sweet music and other diversions. Peasants had to work or starve, and women of all classes were dismissed as hormonally unstable, vulnerable to an attack of the vapours, or susceptible to bad nerves.

An unhappy wife in the nineteenth century often found herself accused of 'hysteria', or womb madness, confined to a dark bedroom for weeks on end, making her condition worse. Even today, women bear the stigma of being less resilient than men and are three times more likely to report symptoms of depression.

Sigmund Freud opted for a 'deep' explanation of depression, tracing its origins to shameful feelings or memories of abuse sublimated in the unconscious, like a boil waiting to be lanced in lengthy sessions with a 'shrink', lasting for several years if necessary.

Freud's division of the mind into surface ego and subterreanean id was dismissed as an unhelpful fiction by the medical profession, and psychoanalysis was ridiculed as the disease to which it purported to be the cure. Doctors preferred pharmaceutical cures, based on clinical trials. Many of these 'wonder drugs' were discovered by accident in the 1950s, but there has been little advance since. More recently psychedelic drugs such as cannabis, magic mushrooms and LSD are being explored for their ability to alleviate symptoms of depression.

From the 1960s onwards, partly as a reaction to the medicalisation of mental illness, there was a shift to humanistic psychology, based on the idea of person-centred 'unconditional positive regard'. For those who found themselves lonely, aimless and feeling small, there were ways to find support, purpose and stature. Many were helped to break free from imprisoning habits of thought and encouraged to get back in touch with their feelings. If they wanted to self-actualise, they needed first to discover who they had it in themselves to be.

Some criticise this approach for being too individualistic and self-centred, creating a me-first culture in which 'let it all hang out' replaced the stiff upper lip of previous generations, who generally complained less. Many 'trippers' disappeared to an ashram in search of their inner child, experimented with rolling in their own excrement or employed a life-style coach.

Though it helps to be told we are special, gifted and important, we also have to learn to pull ourselves up by our own bootstraps, realise it's not all about us, and develop a healthy scepticism about our prospects. Raising our expectations artificially high might not assuage our depression but exacerbate it when we inevitably fall short.

Positive psychology in the 1990s aimed to reset the balance by shifting energy from a self-fulfilling 'despair circuit' in the mind to a future-oriented 'hope circuit'. We need to think affirmatively, aim for a higher purpose and reach out to other people.

Toughening up

The concept of resilience made a dramatic comeback, taking us full circle to the Stoic philosophers of two thousand years ago. Some criticise these ancient sages for being fatalistic killjoys or egotistical pleasure-seekers, but 'being stoical' is about finding the courage to turn troubles into opportunities for growth.

They knew that life cannot be an unbroken run of positives. It comes as given, and there will be times of sadness, loss and bereavement for which we need to prepare ourselves, because we never know what lies ahead. We constantly strive for gain, but we are foolish if we do not simultaneously prepare for loss, using our negative experiences to help us toughen up.

We should learn to control our desires, because they are infinite. We should choose our pleasures carefully, because they are finite. We should distinguish between our wants and our needs, because it is better to want what we have than to complain about not having what we want. Whatever life throws at us, we can make the most of what we are given.

We might not be fully in command of our destiny, but we are masters of our attitude. There's no point bewailing misfortunes that emanate from external events beyond our influence. If a medical problem or an accident leaves us paralysed or disabled, we can't change that, but as Paralympic athletes show, we still have sovereign control of our attitude to our disability.

This applies to the able-bodied too. We need to focus on what we can change, which is our internal reactions to events, and accept what we can't, however unpalatable. We must remove the arrow of suffering from our own heart, not agonising over what is lost in the past or wasting the present moment but being ruggedly optimistic about what is yet to be gained in the future.

The Stoics give tough advice, but they are ruthlessly honest, which is why they appealed to the philosopher Friedrich Nietzsche. He lapsed into madness towards the end of his life, but while he was rational he refused to give way to defeatism and despair. He rejected the comforts of Christianity as cruel delusion and did not wallow in grief. He grabbed life by the throat and lived it enthusiastically with no regrets, declaring that, if offered the chance to go round a second time, he would do so without a second thought.

Viktor Frankl, an Auschwitz survivor, also displayed Stoic virtues. He noted that those who stayed strong during the horror of the Holocaust were those who stayed connected to the needs of others and believed in something beyond their present despair, giving them a 'psychic surplus' which enabled them to cope with the inevitable pain and suffering of the death camps. What mattered was what people did with their pain, which was a question of character.

Some of us enjoy better moral luck than others. If we are subjected to high levels of stress in childhood, we might find ourselves coping less well with set-backs in later life. Early trauma can have lasting impact. Children rescued from Romanian orphanages in 1989, having been denied vital physical contact and emotional attachment in their early years, suffered impaired cognitive and social development.

Viktor Frankl
1905–1997
Frankl survived the Nazi death camps, then used his experience to teach others how to show resilience and find meaning, even where all hope seems to have vanished.

But early setbacks can be overcome. Many of these orphans, showered with love in an adopted family, went on to make remarkable recoveries. Children raised in war zones can go on to be tough, caring individuals who are determined to break the cycle of violence in their own children's lives.

Most of us have the capacity to emerge from trauma to normal functioning, and for everyone who is left an emotional wreck, another emerges psychologically stronger. Being broken can lead to greater long-term resilience, but only if we have the resolve to cast off what is enslaving us.

Seeking happiness

We might think that life owes us joy and success, but happiness is neither a birth-right nor a succession of lucky moments. It is the gift of a life lived well and con-sidered deeply, not a mere surplus of pleasure over pain. It comes not from what we own, or how others rate us, but from how we connect with those around us.

THE STUPENDOUS STORY OF US

It is only tangentially connected to having a good time because it flows not from desire, which can never be satisfied, but from contentment, which is being pleased with what we have.

The minute we think we have happiness in our grasp it is likely to vanish, because it is a passing-place on our journey, not a final destination. We find it when we are least looking for it, such as changing a dirty nappy in the middle of the night, arranging a surprise party, idling in the countryside or completing a difficult task. We can have the toughest job on the planet, perhaps going months without a day off. What makes us happy is knowing we are doing something that matters to us, or that helps others to flourish.

We can't feel positive or be cheerful all the time, but laughter certainly helps. Alongside other 'natural highs' such as falling in love and dancing it stimulates the production of nerve growth factor, which in turn triggers neurogenesis, or the making of new cells in our brain.

An added bonus is that, when we crack our face into a smile, things begin to look and feel better. A belly laugh makes us positively delirious, because our emotions and moods often come *after* what is going on in our body, not before. It's hard to be angry with someone who has just made us grin, and in the mating game, a good sense of humour is worth more than a sexy body. Both attract a partner, but our spirit of play lasts longer. It makes us pleasant to be with, keeps us creative, and gives us a focus outside of ourselves.

It also keeps us balanced and kind. Laughing *at* others is an act of ridicule which merely confirms our prejudices, but laughing *with* each other strengthens the values we hold in common, keeps things in proportion, shakes us out of our ill-humour and releases feel-good endorphins in our bloodstream. Most positive of all is to laugh at ourselves, because that helps us to see where we need to change.

10 What do we value?

Values, feelings, justice, goodness, truth and beauty.

This is my truth – tell me yours. *Aneurin Bevan*

> *Our values are not subjective whims but objective realities,
> fundamental to living good and meaningful lives.*

Choosing our values

Justice, goodness, truth and beauty have long been cherished ideals, not just about how the world is but how we could make it better. In ancient times, there was little agreement whether they are divine commands, unchanging essences, natural features of the cosmos or human inventions for oiling the wheels of society.

Whatever values are, they are not vague abstractions, because we all have 'skin in the game'. They do not come into the world perfectly formed, or as objective facts, but are shaped into mutually supportive 'moral facts' by our actions and confirmed by our feelings. They then inform everything we do, written into our beliefs, intentions and ambitions, which are embedded in our social existence. Choosing to live a meaningful life is our greatest value judgment, and to declare that we possess no values at all is itself a value statement.

Sceptics might point out that more 'justice' has been brought about for humanity by life-saving vaccines than any debate in a legal chamber or philosophical seminar. And yet justice is an authentic reality, both inside our head and as part of the fabric of everyday life, as we discover when we steal someone's parking space.

What do we base these values on? Whether we believe there is providence in the fall of a sparrow or that we are on our own in a vast universe, we have to decide whether to live exclusively for pleasure or toil for the greater good. If we choose the latter, we need reasons for believing that we are morally indebted to others.

Reason might not however be the right place to look. We are not like Mr Spock, rationally dissecting our every thought and coolly calculating our every action. Reason is not the final arbiter of our choices, because our decisions are made further down in our brain, where emotion resides.

We are animals at heart, of a piece with the rest of nature, and members of a tribe called humans, as Charles Darwin reminded us. He collected images of facial expressions from all cultures, concluding that basic emotions such as happiness, sadness, anger, fear, surprise and disgust are recognisable from Amazonians to Zambians, with many variations in between.

Powerful and universal as these default emotions are however, they still do not lead us to the mother lode of our values. Emotions evolved as attention-grabbing biological reactions to be read from the outside. They are signals of approval or warning, not instructions about how to behave or what to believe.

Our values are based on what is going on inside, and this is where feelings come in, as personal responses to what strikes our senses. Without feelings we can't turn data into meaning or drives into purposes. We can't choose between pasta and pacifism, or more importantly understand how others might arrive at different values from us.

We use the words value and worth to signify cost as well as to declare what we care about, but the price of a car, which will depreciate, does not inflame our passions as much as our favourite piece of woodland, which is priceless. In economic terms trees are worthless until chopped down for timber. They then acquire exchange value, as dead lumber, but at the cost of their true value, which is our enjoyment of them as part of a living system that we can bequeath to our children.

The philosopher David Hume remarked that without feelings, he had no way to choose between biting his thumb and destroying the world. We know that he chose to preserve the world, because his friends spoke of him fondly. He was an atheist, but he did not need belief in God to give him reasons to act amicably or charitably. He derived his values from his natural feelings, not a set of religious commandments. He cared because he was human.

Practical ideals

Whatever our religious beliefs, justice, goodness, truth and beauty have long been considered causes worth fighting for because they are based on thousands of generations of wise judgments. If we are wronged we expect the even-handed protection of law. Parents need an achievable model of goodness to offer their children. Disputants need a testable version of truth-telling. Beauty appeals because it is an outward and visible sign of inward and spiritual health.

Plato promoted justice, goodness, truth and beauty as golden ideals in a higher realm, as distinct from the sullied versions we are offered by the messy business of the world. We see though a glass darkly, but if we know what we seek we can access a reality beyond appearances.

His disciple Aristotle, aware that most of us don't have X-ray vision, took a more utilitarian view. We start from a low base, but if we cultivate virtues such as patience, courage, honesty and generosity, we can gradually draw nearer to a world that is more just, good, truthful and beautiful.

Scientists ignore such philosophical musings because they want something that can be studied empirically, chiming with the physics and biology of the actual world. No scientist however can conduct meaningful research without seeking just methods, good outcomes, reliable truths and beautiful explanations. What use is a scientific theory that is not true, does not lead to the greater good, or does not mirror the harmony of the cosmos?

In that sense justice, goodness, truth and beauty are real properties of the cosmos that scientists study, not just subjective hunches but universal backstops for everything they can know and believe. This means that the pronouncements of scientists are as value-laden as any artist, historian or philosopher, and certainly not value-free. They may claim that their values yield better results, but they are values nonetheless.

Consider for instance the debate surrounding the unravelling of the secrets of human genetics. Describing genes as 'selfish' is a useful metaphor for explaining single traits, such as why genes for brown eyes achieve dominance over blue or green.

At the level of the organism however, the cells of the 'body politic' have to cooperate if they are to survive. When these bodies join forces as communities of individuals, they find that the virtue of mutuality is a better long-term strategy than the vice of self-interest. Bullies might thrive temporarily, but the arc of evolution is towards justice, goodness, truth and beauty.

Fighting for justice

We know instinctively as children when something doesn't feel fair, and as adults we readily champion the cause of justice. This suggests that it always seems just beyond our reach, but always worth fighting for. We arrive at this conclusion not by mathematical calculation but in answer to a deep intuition about what is right and fair.

On the savannah justice was focused on the wellbeing and survival of the group, forming the basis of what we call natural law. If someone has shared a kill with me, I am morally bound to reciprocate. If I steal from you, I must make restitution several times over. If I kill one of the clan, I must pay the blood price.

This notion of an eye for an eye, or the law of retaliation, is as old as time itself. Vengeance is a natural instinct, but as the adage goes, when fighting monsters we must beware of becoming monsters ourselves. The evildoer must suffer, but for the victim mercy and forgiveness can be redemptive, avoiding the second injustice of a lifetime of hatred and anger. Seen in the long view, the laws we pass mirror our ideals of the kind of people we want to be.

The glimmerings of such future-oriented thinking are seen in the Code of Hammurabi, written nearly four thousand years ago, reckoned to be the first set of systematic laws. Its core assumptions are that the scales of justice must be evenly balanced, and if the state assumes administration of the law, there is no need for citizens to take the law into their own hands, precipitating generations of resentment. Without the rule of law, there can be no justice, for rich and poor alike.

Nature cannot be our guide in framing human laws, because animals don't kill each other for money or revenge. Humans do, and Hammurabi's achievement was to realise that law delivered without favour draws a line under each offence, allowing victims to feel that a tear in the fabric of society has been mended. He also spared a thought for criminals: punishment must be proportional, fitting the crime.

In the Old Testament we start to hear a more personal note in the dispensation of justice. Prophets rage against the injustice of a child being allowed to die through lack of food or help for the family. We are given more humane definitions of justice, not as retribution but as mediation, restoration and redistribution. We are told we should judge not, lest we be judged.

As an absolute ruler Hammurabi was the voice of authority, and he had henchmen to enforce his will. State law doesn't feel so 'natural' when we are obliged on pain of death to worship the emperor, pay heavy taxes or join the military.

Even today, not all laws are freedom-preserving, and in many states, the rights of the individual are regularly sacrificed to the national interest. As a rule, we don't object to paternalistic laws which limit freedom only for the greater good, such as the compulsory wearing of seat belts. We react less favourably to moralising laws which tell us how we should live, such as declaring gay marriage or abortion to be illegal.

In liberal societies we take 'justice for all' as a birthright: the law will defend us from arbitrary torture, unlawful arrest, confiscation of property, denial of a fair trial, crooked judges and wrongful imprisonment. It cannot however guarantee social justice. For that, we have to look to our collective conscience.

Common law is made by judges in local courts, sustaining a tradition of fair judgments that have stood the test of time, whereas positive law is put into place by legislators. Both traditions have strengths, but if we are not to be locked in the mindset of a bygone age, or stuck with antiquated laws which perpetuate established injustices, we need laws which can adapt quickly to new needs and circumstances.

It makes sense for instance to update laws which protect freedom of expression on a regular basis and to persist in repealing those which enshrine the right of every citizen to have a gun in the home, if only because weapons too readily find themselves in the hands of criminals, psychopaths and children.

The law is theoretically blind to colour, class and money, but however tightly worded and codified, it is a human affair, and so open to interpretation. Constant interrogation and vigilance are required if the scales of justice and mercy are to be kept evenly weighted.

This calls for important safeguards. We know that dictatorship is in the offing when due process is denied, or judges are threatened or hand-picked for their political views. Lawmakers must be democratically elected, judges must be representative of the people they serve and society must policed by consent. Where we enjoy these things, it is easy to become complacent about the benefits of this separation of powers, but if we live in a police state, we realise how vital it is.

Trying to be good

Goodness is as slippery a concept as justice, changing with the times and difficult to define. Saying that good equals what we desire or what makes us feel better is a circular argument, and naively assuming that everything works for the greater good is not borne out by brute fact.

The Ancient Greeks preoccupied themselves with living the good life, but this was almost exclusively focused on their own flourishing, barely sparing a thought for slaves, women, the destitute or barbarians who couldn't speak Greek.

THE STUPENDOUS STORY OF US

We usually equate goodness with rightness, but sometimes a good intention can have a bad consequence, which doesn't feel right at all. A law banning assisted dying, based on the sanctity of life, can oblige us to end our life in pain, when we have expressly requested while in our right mind for this not to happen.

In the legal world, this is known as a hard case, which more often than not leads to bad law. Legislators can declare that euthanasia is illegal, but they can't wrangle with us how prolonged suffering can ever be good. As in the human heart, goods often conflict or are incommensurate, making it hard to do the right thing. How do we square the circle of valuing life at all costs, seeking the least harm, honouring the dying person's wishes and doing what is best for the patient?

The bombing of Hiroshima in 1945 shows how a terrible wrong can be justified as an overall right. For every civilian death, it is believed that another eight lives would have been lost in protracted conventional warfare if the war had been allowed to drag on, possibly for another two years. Sometimes we have to do bad in order to do good.

So what makes us yearn for the good in the first place? Did evolution, God or our desire to control our baser instincts put it in us in the form of conscience? We certainly need the pricks of guilt and shame because we have every reason to be afraid of the demons of our own nature, and it is naive to suppose that evil is merely the absence of good. No other species is capable of the horrors of Oradour, My Lai and the Killing Fields. These were not natural evils, like earthquakes, but moral atrocities committed by rational agents who were free to choose otherwise.

Our ancestors must have leaned more towards good than bad, otherwise we wouldn't be here. This glib assumption does not however make the contradictions of goodness any simpler to resolve. The principal difficulty is that goodness is a moveable feast. What is good for me isn't necessarily good for you. What seems good today might not look quite so good tomorrow. It is good to be free to eat burgers and buns every day, but it won't feel so good when we're overweight and struggling for breath.

Moralists proclaim a Golden Rule of treating others as we would wish them to treat us, but they can't help us make specific ethical choices about whether to give our money to the poor, invest it in renewable energy or splash out on that sports car we've always dreamed of owning.

Religious teachers urge us to be good but they can't find an objective grounding for goodness, or tell us whether we are naturally good or evil. They can't explain whether we behave ourselves because we feel God is constantly watching us, or because we freely choose to do the right thing. They can't account for the presence of evil in a world made by a good God, or give us a version of evil that is not merely their definition of sin.

We like to simplify our moral choices by demonising our enemies: we are good and saintly, they are evil and monstrous. But no criminal is wholly evil, and no saint is totally pure. We are all complex moral mixes, and if we are good in any sense, it is because the better angels of our nature have somehow flourished, often against the odds.

For centuries people who prided themselves on their goodness also accepted slavery without question. We might think we're better than they were, but we continue to pollute the planet, and we unwittingly acquiesce in the idea of torture being carried out in our name, albeit by security forces operating far away and out of sight.

Telling the truth

Truth, like goodness, is a chameleon which changes colour according to its background. The Ancient Greeks saw it as constantly present but hidden behind the veil of our ignorance. Socrates warned that tearing back the curtain could be unsettling, but a price worth paying for self-knowledge. Plato wanted the truth to bolster the social order, so he supported the idea of the Noble Lie: the state and its laws are effective only if we don't question them as power structures that keep us in place. The Sophists twisted truth to their own convenience and the Sceptics doubted whether it existed at all.

No wonder our modern concept of truth boils down to what works, or what we have no reason to doubt. We go on the evidence temporarily before us, but given the vagaries of our perceptual apparatus, this is a risky strategy. Our white bed sheets can look black in the middle of the night. In that sense, all truths are contingent, or dependent on other things being equal, especially the truths of love and life which we have to meet half way and make for ourselves.

'The sun rises in the east' is an analytic truth which doesn't require our say-so to be true for everyone, even when we're all asleep in bed. 'I will love you until death do us part' is a synthetic truth, true only for me right now, at least until I become disenchanted or meet someone else.

Mathematicians by contrast see their truths as necessary and eternal, as if written in bold letters across the sky. Two plus two equals four anywhere in any universe. If we start with certain axioms, our conclusions will follow automatically.

Even in logic however, truth is not always self-evident or neatly algorithmic. Unless we can spot the flaw in the syllogism 'Socrates is a man, Socrates has an ugly face, therefore all men have ugly faces', we might find ourselves drawn from faulty premises to dangerous conclusions about race, class and gender.

Scientists bank on the fact that particles behave similarly in every hadron collider in the world, but they have to be more cautious than mathematicians and logicians in their pursuit of truth. New knowledge might surprise them, forcing a revision of long-held theories. Even the truths of science are provisional and probabilistic, based on inference to the best explanation given the facts currently in front of us.

Old truths constantly face new tests. It once seemed impossible that a sailing vessel could travel twice as fast as the speed of the wind, but with the invention of the lateen sail this became the case. Modern physicists have not observed anything travelling faster than the speed of light, at least not in our patch of the universe, but if they do, Einstein's theories will have to be rewritten.

Scientists are not troubled by new knowledge because, unlike religious believers, they don't claim revealed or eternal truth. They have to decode how the world actually works, not speculate about how they would like it to work. They can never be certain, so they regard their fallibility as the best guarantee of getting closer and closer to the probable truth of how matter behaves.

Rather than claiming perfect truth, they opt instead for models of reality that are elegant and beautiful, but even this presents risks. One ugly fact can force a rethink, especially in the pursuit of the fabled Theory of Everything. So far this seems to comprise not a single truth but interlocking fragments of complementary truths.

The uneasy balance between certainty and doubt applies even more strongly to the personal realm. We can't look to our memories for documentary truth, because we rewrite them every time we recall them. Nor does life fit neatly into binary notions of true or false. Most of our decisions are clouded by vested interests, bobbling around somewhere in what logicians call 'the excluded middle'.

In what is known as the correspondence theory of truth, we expect the facts of reality to match the evidence of our senses: I saw three ships a-sailing by, not two or four. But we also expect our truths to cohere: ships sail only in a world where sailors know the ropes and how to read the waves.

Religious teachers can't claim that their truths correspond to objective realities, so they opt for truth as coherence. We can't *see* 'God is Love' with our physical eyes, but if we accept it as a fundamental principle that underpins creation, everything else falls into place, including the presence of evil in the world. Science has to start from the opposite end, pursuing truth as correspondence: something is true if and only if the facts fit the observations, and the theories have been tested to destruction.

Given these uncertainties, honest doubt and constant questioning are the best policy, in both science and life. We never just 'see', because our brain is not a mere recording device or camera. We perceive what we have become accustomed to see, filtered through the lens of experience and culture. Sometimes our senses deceive us, or new measuring instruments help us to see the previously unseen.

What we accept as orthodoxy today might turn out to be untrue tomorrow, a possibility that scientists find disturbing but have to acknowledge. There is always the chance that we are plain wrong, or right for the wrong reasons. Something might happen which causes us to abandon beliefs that have served us well for centuries.

Buddha
6th century BCE
Statues of the Buddha invariably show him with his eyes closed. Having emptied his mind of distracting thoughts, he is free to see justice, goodness, truth and beauty with his inner eye.

Truth is grounded in fact. Some facts we have to take on trust from accredited sources, but where we can, we must do our own fact-checking. If we are lazy, or seek out only facts which fit our prejudices, it will be like going to a railway station and waiting on a randomly chosen platform for the next train to anywhere. If we don't know where we are going, we won't be able to verify the stops along the way. We will arrive with false beliefs about the world, with no way of checking them.

If the facts change en route we must change our opinion, but this is hard. Our brain struggles to embrace a new reality and changing our mind can feel like a threat to our identity, because truth is as much about feeling as intellect. We become wedded to our worldview, our 'take' not just on how the world works, but on how we think it *should* work, from the perspective of our particular life and experience.

This makes our mindset more of an ideology than a theory, neither verifiable nor falsifiable, formed in our teens while our brain configuration is fluid and we are making up our mind on life's important issues. After that, we become known for what we believe, and when pushed to account for our beliefs, all we can do is point to prior beliefs, which take us full circle back to our feelings and values.

This means we are bound to disagree on important issues with those around us. Facts alone won't settle our disputes because they are value-ridden and useless without interpretation. There will inevitably be awkward differences of opinion because the things that matter most to us are highly contestable *because* they matter. The good news is that we can agree to disagree.

If we take time to verify our sources, we might arrive at what the Buddha called 'right opinion' based on justified true belief, remembering the old journalistic principle that we are entitled to our opinions, but not to our facts. Comment is free, but facts are sacred.

In the nineteenth century John Stuart Mill championed open debate so that truth could flourish in the public arena. He resisted any notion of banning unorthodox views, even if blatantly false, because he believed that in a fair contest, truth will always prevail because it is right.

He knew that we can't make something true merely by the strength of our belief, we can't claim absolute certainty, and we can't insist that *our* truth is truer than everyone else's. All we can say is that, up to the present point, we have no reason *not* to believe what we consider to be true, accepting that we may well be mistaken about our convictions.

Mill's liberalism has not alas fared well in the internet age, where truth faces some very dangerous competition, such as millions of false facts being pumped out by bots at the press of a button. Another difficulty unaccounted for by his rationalism is that we are such good liars. We are economical with the truth, not because we set out to tell deliberate falsehoods but because we are human, and truth is often ambiguous. We have secrets to hide, punishments to avoid, contracts to win and ourselves to deceive.

Mill's views on toleration still however carry weight. Rather than burn a book it is better to argue long and hard in the public arena why we disagree with it so strongly, and demand that its author respond. There are two good reasons for this. Firstly, there will be *some* truth in it, which we need to acknowledge. Secondly, before we know it, our own book will be on the bonfire.

Sometimes the truth is best not told, such as when we put compassion before truth at the bedside of a dying friend. That doesn't mean that we have lost sight of truth, because we know how much honesty matters in our dealings with each other. We also hate the awful feeling we get when we discover we've been lied to.

Plato dismissed art and fiction for telling us lies, but he underestimated our need for them. They are true lies, because they tell us emotional truths. We dismiss them when they don't 'ring true' because we come equipped with a natural facility for living with ambiguous truths, and a strong sense of when we are being duped.

We apply no less exacting standards to our history books, becoming rightfully angry when the past is distorted or hidden from us. Lies are far more likely to be sold to us as truths in official 'factual' accounts of reality than in any work of the imagination.

If we want to know the 'truth' of history, we can do so only through the lens of the 'truth' of the present, which calls for empathy, insight and not a little hard work. The truths of history are time-bound and culture-bound, and to presume otherwise is to lapse into thinking ahistorically. Those who pull down the statues of leaders revered in their day must accept that later generations might come gunning for them.

Appreciating beauty

And so we come finally to beauty, which seems on the surface to be merely ornamental and cosmetic, but is more integral to our survival than we think. Our pattern-seeking brain is drawn to fineness of form not just as a guide to the health and fitness of a potential partner, but also as a promise of a fairer and happier future.

This ideal is perhaps best captured in Leonardo's illustration of Vitruvian Man, drawn around 1490. The outstretched limbs of a Christ-like figure in crucifix pose touching the edges of a perfect circle show man made in the image of a god.

Our standard of beauty changes through history and within our own development because it lies in our shifting eyes, as perceived by our mercurial mind. This does not mean that beauty is a fleeting will-o'-the-wisp. We cannot conceive of a world without art, and there are many cultural variations of what is perceived to be beautiful which leave real footprints in the brains of their beholders.

Our appreciation of the beautiful, as of the world itself, is at first sensual: we must touch, taste and smell the cherries. If we stay in thrall to such pleasures, or indulge them to excess, we run the risk of dying before our time. Better the frugal gourmet than the bloated gourmand.

Beauty invites us to discriminate more subtly between our sensory delights. Pleasures are mere signals to the brain and temporary cessations of pain, but if we learn to refine our responses to them we can admire texture, colour and form aesthetically, in our imagination, without the need for sensory stimulus. As the saying goes in the art world, when an ass stares at a painting it should not expect to see an angel looking back.

In this vein we find the nude beautiful, not because it is sexually stimulating but because it reveals to us the beauty of the human form as an ideal, transcending momentary pleasure. The Romantics were attracted to grand vistas as glimpses of the sublime, their overwhelming beauty beyond human comprehension. We find hand-crafted objects beautiful and worth keeping, even if they show the signs of age, because they connect us to their maker. Mass-produced objects, however sleek or glossy, end up in the recycle bin.

We each perceive beauty differently, and if everything looks alike to us, the fault is not in the world but in our dull eyes. Mathematicians see the perfection of beauty in the elegance of their theorems, artists in the ratio of the golden section, scientists in the magic of reality, petrolheads in the raw power of a racing car, and religious believers in the love of God. Older couples see it in each other, because they still see the glow of youth in each other's eyes.

Mother Theresa saw not decay and disfigurement in the faces of the lepers she worked with in Calcutta but an imperishable inner beauty visible only to the mind, which sees more than the eye. It's one thing to admire the beauty of the lotus, another to discern loveliness in the mud that nourishes it.

There is no simple formula for deciding what makes art beautiful. There must be consonance of parts and skilled composition as in a fine flower arrangement, which is a dressed-up version of nature. In ikebana, or Japanese floral art, our eye is drawn to the spaces between, because what is left out can be as important as what is included.

Nor can we easily decide the worth of beauty because we prize it as an end in itself, requiring no other justification. We are prepared to pay more for a bunch of roses than a bunch of nettles, but what about a painting of nettles signed by

Georgia O'Keefe, or a doodle of absolutely nothing at all by John Lennon? A bit of 'found art' gains value just by being hung in a gallery or purchased by a millionaire, just as cheap wine tastes better when served from expensive bottles.

We marvel at a mountain sunset, but we don't see the life and death struggles played out on its slopes. We are awed by the magnificence of a cathedral, but we overlook the century of toil by generations of workers who donated their last mite to make it happen. We are appalled but fascinated by the terrible beauty of a regiment of soldiers marching up the line to their death.

We forget that beauty can corrupt the innocent mind, lure us into distorted notions of eugenic perfection, torture the jilted lover or torment the young girl starving herself to conform to an impossible body image. Hitler was a lover of beauty, stealing hundreds of works of art to sate his appetite, but this was of no consolation to the millions who died to satisfy his kleptomania.

For art to engage our intellect and feelings in equal measure, there must be moral as well as aesthetic intent, perhaps a revelation of the beauty in simple things or a vision of a better world that we wish we could experience more intensely. It might also shock and disturb us as a way of peeling the scales from our eyes, or show us how we can live our own life as a work of art.

As we head towards an increasingly technocratic future, nothing will make sense except in the light of justice, goodness, truth and beauty. They are fundamental values for what it means to be human, and we will struggle to survive without them.

11 How do we stay healthy?

The body, diet, exercise, sleep, nervous system, hormones, pain, inflammation, mental health, companionship, ageing, meditation.

You should pray for a healthy mind in a healthy body. *Juvenal, Roman poet*

> *We enjoy our best health when we listen carefully to the constant conversation between our mind and body.*

Listening to our body

Until quite recent times, if we were ill and could afford a doctor, we were likely to be subjected to bleedings, purges and mercury treatments which were more likely to kill than cure. As late as the twentieth century doctors still saw us as bodies vulnerable to contagion or bags of bones that needed the occasional repair. Their workshop manual had little to say about our mind which was regarded as its own place, a mystery beyond the remit of medical practice.

Slowly an older model of healthcare is returning: we are complex coalitions of body and mind. We say we *have* cancer, as if our body has betrayed us, but when we are troubled with an illness of the mind we say we *are* depressed, autistic or prone to panic attacks. These conditions are so engrossing that we cannot tell the dancer from the dance.

With this 'whole person' approach in mind, the motto of a healthy mind in a healthy body has been resurrected. We are psycho-biological organisms, capable of ministering to ourselves. By paying our mind and body equal attention we can not only better manage our fears, longings and disappointments but also be stronger at fending off bugs and illnesses.

Interoception helps us to listen to what our body is telling us and regulate our upsets. How well is our liver coping with yesterday's over-indulgence, did we get a good night's sleep, do we still have a twinge in our knee, how steadily is our heart beating today? Evidence suggests that the more simpatico our mind and body, the lower our risk of anxiety, depression and insomnia.

It works the other way round too. Complaints such as ulcers and eczema are often the side-effects of a troubled mind. On its own a thought is weightless and powerless, but as part of an organic system it can effect physical changes in us, as we discover when we think of an ice cream on a sunny afternoon.

Witch doctors in times gone by realised they had only to place in our mind the *idea* of being cursed to send our body into irreversible shutdown. Nowadays, by the same token, a bad prognosis can send us into a downwards spiral. We are highly suggestible and if we are convinced we are ill the symptoms are not long behind.

It works the other way too. Hearing our doctor say 'You're perfectly fine' can sometimes be therapy enough, because merely believing something will make us better can help us to self-cure by switching on healing properties in our body and quietening the pain centres in our brain, even when we know it's a placebo, or medicine that is chemically inert. The power of morphine as a painkiller is enhanced if we are told we are being given it, and it is going to reduce our suffering.

Our use of language reveals the intimate bond between our mind and body. We feel our way forward, give each other the cold shoulder, get butterflies in our stomach, keep a stiff upper lip and avoid anal personalities. Squaring our shoulders can make us feel more confident about facing the world. When we are unwell we welcome the healing power of touch, and when we breathe deeply we feel calmer.

Exercising and eating

Exercise is an excellent way of keeping mind and body in harmony, and its medical benefits are overwhelming. Our brain stays younger, energy levels feel higher, blood pressure is lower, blood sugars are reduced, circulation is improved, joints stay more supple, inflammation is kept in check, cell metabolism is stimulated, and damaging toxins are flushed through the system. An active lifestyle also maintains levels of osteocalcin, a protein which keeps our bones strong, especially necessary as we age.

We don't have to run a marathon or achieve Olympian levels of fitness to stay in trim, only get our heart rate up for thirty minutes a day and move regularly, perhaps by walking the dog, sweeping the path or using the stairs instead of the lift. For gym-bunnies, strength training can reduce anxiety levels and increase self-confidence, but a mix of resistance and endurance activities seems to give the best all-round effects.

Cold water swimming or diving into snow after a sauna kick-starts our whole system into survival mode. So does a brief bout of high intensity training, perhaps because it reprises our ancestors' stop-start lifestyle on the savannah. The chase of the hunt was followed by a long spell of rest during which they moved around freely or performed light activities, never sitting for too long.

This balance matters because we evolved to be on the move and predominantly upright when awake, allowing gravity to do its work on our muscles and cardio-vascular system. Sitting for long periods thickens the walls of our arteries, despite a good base level of fitness. Even fidgeting helps to keep our system alert, so couch potatoes take note.

We are also connected to our biological past through our gut. We evolved as omnivores, eating meat on the rare occasions it was available, but consuming more cereal crops and dairy foods as we drifted from hunter-gathering to arable farming and cattle herding. The so-called paleo diet was not therefore heavy on meat-eating. Our ancestors were just as likely to be vegetarian because plants are plentiful, and apart from lacking sufficient vitamin B12 they are as nutritious and energy-giving as meat.

Our gut has had hundreds of generations to adjust to this mixed diet, its flora of bacteria outnumbering the cells in our body. They are attuned to our genome and what's on the menu locally, which explains why we get tummy upsets when we travel.

The important lesson about our ancestors' diet is not what they ate, but how they ate. When a fresh kill came in, they scoffed a lot at one sitting while the meat was fresh, then went back to light grazing for several days. This habit of 'gorge and starve' led to the 'thrifty gene' hypothesis: our body automatically stores energy for slow release when times get hard.

The problem for modern eaters is that we tend to 'gorge and gorge', usually on food from which many of the good things have been taken out by industrial processing, and a lot of bad things added. One tip for avoiding over-eating is to eat slowly, allowing our stomach time to tell our brain when it is full. Eating with other people also helps because we pause to talk between mouthfuls.

We need carbohydrates, but fasting to restrict calorie intake every so often can literally take the weight off our feet, as well as help to stimulate the growth of new neurons in our brain. Cells that go hungry for a while suffer less damage to their DNA, living longer as a result. Crash diets tend to be counterproductive because our body's response is to go into shock mode, then glut itself with replacement calories at the first opportunity.

We are told to watch our fat consumption, but not all fats are harmful, and not all obese people are unhealthy. Several studies show that dairy fats can lower risk of cardiovascular disease and also protect against type 2 diabetes. Nor is there evidence that eggs raise levels of 'bad' cholesterol in our blood. We can eat as many as we like.

We are warned against excess salt and sugar which were rare treats on the savannah, but modern processed foods are full of them, taste-engineered to make us keep eating, potentially opening the door to heart disease, cancer and diabetes. We are advised to avoid refined grains which go straight through us, opting instead for fibre-rich whole-foods which do a better job of regulating our appetite, aiding our digestion and cleansing our gut. White bread, sugar and rice sound pure, but only because they have had all their natural brown goodness bleached out. 'Five a day' of fruit and vegetables is good advice, so long as they are fresh, and not predominantly fruit, which ups our sugar levels.

Dieting is a big industry, but most of its marketing overlooks some simple truths. None of us is average, and two people can digest the same meal in quite different ways because we have multiple response systems. Set point theory suggests that we each have an optimum weight, calibrated to our genes, age and lifestyle. Most of us fret about putting on the odd pound or two, but the real time to worry is when our weight plummets unexpectedly.

Obesity is a puzzle to dieticians. It seems that our metabolic rate can be set as early as in the womb. Whatever that may be, it's best not to allow ourselves to become overweight because we might find ourselves locked in a constant fight with our body which is determined to maintain the weight it has become used to, especially after a crash diet.

On the flip side, eating disorders such as anorexia and bulimia have become more common, their causes as complex as their cures, ranging over genetic propensity, distressing mental illness, hormone imbalance, psychological defence mechanism, image consciousness, peer pressure and lifestyle choice, not to mention fashion advertising and fast food marketing.

Allergies and gluten intolerance appear to be on the increase. There are more pollutants in our environment, but ironically, the culprit is not so much what we consume as what we miss out on, especially when we are young. Being shielded from muck and dirt over-protects our immune system, denies our gut 'good' bacteria and prevents us from building up antibodies.

Children brought up on farms, ingesting the occasional piece of cowpat, have the healthiest microbial diversity to act as a foil against infection and ill health. We evolved alongside animals, especially dogs, and sharing their pathogens makes us and them stronger, not weaker.

Sleeping and dreaming

Sleep is the sanctuary where we spend a third of our lives, but it is becoming problematic for many. Good sleep is essential not so much for the body as the brain which needs 'down time' to consolidate the lessons of the day and to flush out toxins.

Babies need to snooze for fourteen hours a day, teenagers for ten and adults eight, even in old age. Chronic lack of sleep eventually impairs our health and performance in our waking hours. Shift workers learn to manage their sleep regime, but 'social jetlag' is a problem for those who burn the candle at both ends, and for teenagers, who not only like to stay up late but are not at their best when the school bell disturbs their slumber.

To sleep, perchance to dream

Shakespeare described sleep as 'chief nourisher in life's feast'. If there is one favour we can do ourselves, it is to ensure that we sleep well, and that we listen to our dreams.

We can break our sleep into shorter spells, so long as we allow time for full cycles of about an hour and a half during which the wave pattern in our brain slows down, causing us to have dreams and nightmares. These don't harm us, because sleep protects us in a psychological safe zone. Nor do we act them out, because our 'motor switch' is off. If it stays on, we're likely to sleepwalk and, in extreme cases, leave the house and commit a crime.

Neuroscientists say that our dreams are caused by our brain doing its house-cleaning. It reverts to the default network, our visual cortex generating random images and flashing them onto the screen of our mind while the attention and executive functions are deactivated. Something similar happens when we day-dream, perhaps up to a hundred times a day.

Therapists urge us to grant much greater import to our dreams, which may contain recurring patterns and symbols which can guide us on our journey through the perilous shoals of life, if we take time to study them. Some of us perfect the art of lucid dreaming, a semi-conscious state in which we can control some of our dream content. Given that we live in age of paranoia and conspiracy theories, keeping in touch with our unconscious might help us to stay sane and maintain mental health.

Insomnia has become a problem for many, its causes more likely to be psychological than organic. If we go to bed stressed, we are less likely to wake up refreshed. If we leave our phone switched on by our pillow, we are not giving our mind the respite it needs. Research shows that going to bed an hour or so before midnight ensures a more refreshing sleep, but if we sleep irregular hours, our body systems become out of kilter, raising the risk of stroke. Sleep well and dream sweetly, because the shorter our sleep, the shorter our life expectancy.

Staying chemically balanced

Most of what goes on inside us is below the radar, regulated by our autonomic nervous system. Unless we jump up and down we're not aware of our heartbeat or blood pressure, and unless we overeat we pay our digestive system no heed.

Our body's health is maintained by self-regulating systems designed to keep us on an even keel, with no conscious input needed. If we get hot we sweat, if we start to dehydrate we get thirsty, if we sleep badly we get tired sooner the next day. In that sense, our body is talking to us all the time.

One of our nervous system's most important jobs is monitoring the flow of hormones through our body, which act as messengers and catalysts. The ones we are most aware of are the sex hormones oestrogen and testosterone, which stimulate big physical changes, starting with the determination of our gender in the womb at six weeks.

Testosterone is sometimes demonised for driving 'warrior' aggression or 'toxic' masculinity, but this is to confuse its biological function with its cultural expression. Little girls get a shot of testosterone and another burst after the menopause. What feminises them is their tenfold larger boost of oestrogen, which allows them to live longer on average than men because it is a natural anti-oxidant. Men don't miss out completely because they get a dose of oestrogen when their libido starts to wane.

Hormones are influencers, not determiners of behaviour, and a man tanked up with testosterone can just as easily choose to become a devoted father or celibate priest. 'Men behaving badly' thrives only in communities that allow macho memes to flourish. The male descendants of Viking berserkers have long subdued the urge to go out on a raping and pillaging spree.

As many as fifty other hormones are regulated by glands spread throughout our body affecting our moods and inclinations, but the complexity of human psychology means that they work their magic only within the context of a considered life. It is too simple to say that dopamine urges us to crave pleasure; it can also make us determined to finish a task. Nor does oxytocin make us fall in love; it can also make us resentful of outsiders.

Serotonin is similarly ambivalent, not always living up to its 'happy hormone' reputation. Male chimpanzees with high serotonin levels become aggressive alphas, while low serotonin males sulk in the background, prone to depression because they can't get access to females. Similar patterns of dominance and submission linked to serotonin levels have been noted in human groups.

Hormones double up as neurotransmitters in the brain, altering the chemistry between our synapses in an instant. When we take a drug of any kind, whether it's a painkiller, alcohol, cannabis or hot chocolate, we are in effect supersizing our hormones. Even what we eat affects our state of mind because the microbes in our stomach are in regular communication with our brain.

Opiates give a big kick because they mimic the action of 'feel good' dopamine, but they are also highly addictive. We can avoid that fate by enjoying the body's natural opiates which come for free with no side effects, provided by the endorphins that lift our mood after exercise, or when we're in good company.

Pain and meaning

Our body speaks most loudly to us through pain, though as with hormones there is no simple nexus between cause and effect. Though we feel pain all over our body its control centre is the brain, which itself feels no pain. It can be operated on without anaesthetic and when we say we have a headache, we are really complaining of inflammation in the protective layers around the brain, not in the brain itself.

To underline how complex and psychological pain can be, some feel pain when there is no underlying cause. Some are injured but feel no pain. Pain can increase or lessen at different times of day, vary in intensity depending on who we are with, 'refer' itself elsewhere in our body, and disappear if we do something to take our minds off it. Some choose pain deliberately, either to prove loyalty to a group or to push the boundaries of enjoyment.

Suffering, bereavement and grief fire the same parts of the brain, which is why we talk of heartache. There may be nothing wrong with our body but the loss of a loved one can make us feel genuine hurt, and the pain can last much longer.

Inflammation is the principal cause of pain throughout the body. Usually it is a defence mechanism to give us time to recover, but occasionally the body can attack itself, mistaking healthy cells for intruders. Our autoimmune system has had millions of years to learn to recognise alien pathogens, or how to coexist with them, but modern life presents us with many new enemy agents, some physical and some psychological, the one aggravating the other. If we're generally run-down we make ourselves especially vulnerable, so we're back to where we started: make sure we are in tune with our body, exercise regularly, eat moderately and sleep soundly.

We also need to work on our relations with others, which serve as a powerful 'social medicine'. Our most earnest desire is to feel at home in the world and we achieve this through our network of family, friends and colleagues. We fear enforced isolation, divorce, redundancy, shunning and exile because they break the delicate threads that hold us together. We crave companionship, which literally means breaking bread with each other.

John Donne reminded us that we are not islands but a part of the continent of mankind. We evolved as social creatures, our physical and mental health deeply connected to the company we keep. If we're lucky our circle of friends includes individuals who not only give us support when we need it, but also show us how to master pain and get through tough times.

Keeping the brain young

The starkest reminder of the mind's dependence on the brain is Alzheimer's disease, causing increasing concern as more of us take advantage of the extra twenty years of life granted us by modern medicine. The price of longer life seems to be degenerative disease. We expect wear and tear of our body and our brain similarly slows down, but we can generally mask this because an older brain has learned many more tricks.

Dementia is harder to hide because discrete areas of the brain begin to die off, inducing a 'brain fog' in which each victim suffers uniquely. Names become harder to recall, words become elusive, well-known faces turn into strangers and images no longer make sense in the visual cortex. Childhood memories are often the last to go, because they are buried deepest in the brain.

All is not doom and gloom however, or a miserable descent to the grave. The brains of some eighty-year olds are sharper than those a quarter of their age, aided by a lifetime's learning of short-cuts and wisdom. In other studies, happiness levels seem highest in this age group.

The seeds of brain disease are often sown in our thirties and forties, so the sensible money is on prevention. Research shows that children brought up with books in the home grow up with greater resilience to cognitive decline. Our gut often acts as a second brain, so maintaining a healthy microbiome can stave off dementia. There is much therefore that we can do to keep our brain young and healthy, whatever our biological age, avoiding degeneration, mutation, inflammation and the build-up of damaging plaque in our synapses. Like the body, our brain is a machine that can be oiled and maintained.

The advice about exercise, diet and sleep applies all through our life, and certainly shouldn't stop at retirement. We can keep busy, take up skydiving, learn new skills, sustain friendship circles and get involved in local initiatives. All of these help to stimulate our white and grey matter into our twilight years and keep our body strong.

We might choose to put our trust in transfusions of 'young blood', implants of genes from animals that don't seem to age or freezing our brain until a cure is found. These however are unproven therapies, and there is no point in living forever if we've lost our teeth, taste and eyes. Growing old enjoyably grasping every opportunity to learn and socialise seems the best option.

As highly successful ways of integrating body and mind, and following the decline of traditional faith, meditation and mindfulness have become popular spiritual exercises for all ages. Their aim is not withdrawal from the world, out-of-body enlightenment, mystical insight or seeing with a 'third eye'. For some it is quiet contemplation of philosophy and life, for others it is more intensive engagement with what is around them.

Depending how much time we are prepared to spend and which tradition we choose, mindfulness and meditation can offer physical benefits of lower stress levels, reduced fear centres in our brain, higher resistance to pain and more alert cognition, without any need for religious belief.

More broadly, they can deepen our perception, make us feel better connected to each other and show us how to enter more fully into the present moment. Life often drifts casually by, so it's good at any age to reflect on our passions by stepping out of time for a moment.

'Time out' is always welcome, but emptying our mind of distractions is a difficult discipline, and unsettling for some. Many of us are content with the reality we have and don't crave unity with the cosmos, but shutting down our frenetic 'top brain' for a while and taking time to explore our inner world has to be worth a try.

If we find meditation and mindfulness too cerebral we can turn to yoga, which has long reminded us that we have a body as well as a mind. True to its meaning, it 'yokes together' our body awareness with our mental wellbeing. Massage in its many forms can also act as a destressant and detoxicant, calming our thoughts, stimulating our internal organs, lowering our blood pressure and increasing our circulation.

The word health denotes not just what is listed on our medical record. It comes from the same root as feeling whole and holy, not to mention hale and hearty. Rather than buying the latest fitness tracker or allowing ourselves to be medicalised, we might choose instead to go for a gentle ramble with a friend, reflecting on the things that matter to both of us, stretching our legs, grabbing a lungful of air and taking time to notice the changes going on inside, between and around us.

12 Why is freedom fundamental?

Freedom, fate, predestination, liberty, democracy, responsibility, agency, libertarianism, free speech, determinism, free will, nudge theory, conformity, imagination, neuroplasticity.

Stone walls do not a prison make. *Richard Lovelace*

> *Thought is free, but actions have consequences.*

The bounds of freedom

'I'm free' sang Roger Daltry in the 1975 rock musical 'Tommy'. Did he think he was casting off the negative impositions of political repression and social convention, or was he welcoming the positive freedoms of thinking for himself and singing in a rock band?

Faced by the brute necessity of getting to the end of each day, debates about freedom meant nothing to our ancestors. As society became more hierarchical their choice shrank even further. The thousands of labourers toiling on the Pyramids had no alternative but to turn up for work every day or face severe punishment. Modern totalitarian governments reduce their citizens to mere biological existence by putting the needs of the state above the autonomy of the individual. As in an ant colony, there is no thought of freedom or existence outside the collective.

Autocrats insist that we are most free when we live in accord with their laws, but freedom for the few built on repression of the many is no freedom at all. In fascist regimes the tinder of ideas, which are the spark of opposition, is extinguished by the tyranny of the blood. Liberal societies work the other way round: the state has to be strong in order to uphold the laws that protect individual freedom. Anarchists see any laws as a form of imprisonment, but civil society would collapse if we all lived off-grid in the swamps.

Freedom cannot be absolute because unbridled freedom licenses the wolf to terrorise the lambs. Nor can there be total freedom of speech. We have no right to defame those we don't like or impose a speaking ban on them simply because we find their views offensive. The law defends us against slander, but not against hearing things we don't agree with.

If we have signed the Official Secrets Act it is a bold and dangerous act to betray the activities of the deep state, however justified we feel. In times of emergency or terrorist threat, draconian laws are passed to monitor and control the flow of information. These seem justified at the time, but when the crisis passes we find ourselves handcuffed by our own restrictions, our freedom not enhanced but diminished. We have bought a bit of extra security at the cost of some valuable freedoms, and a freedom lost is difficult to regain.

Censorship poses many challenges to civil liberties and freedom of expression. By what power can anyone limit what we are free to say? No-one has a monopoly on knowledge or is entitled to blank what we choose to think. Who censors them? The opposite of censorship is toleration, but that raises questions too. Who is to tell us what we must tolerate, or what to do when we are confronted with the intolerable?

None of these awkward questions matters if we believe that fate holds sway over our destiny. Today we resist the idea that we have to tolerate what the gods throw at us, but our ancestors knew that famine, war and pestilence were going to come their way eventually. Resigning themselves to the inevitable was less distressing than living in a state of continual dread. They were stoical in their attitude, wrestling only with those issues where their actions could make a difference.

Given that life was in the main nasty, brutish and short, the major religions of the world tried to justify life's grimness, at best offering consolation in the next world. In the East karma was presented as an inescapable burden, transferred like a criminal record from one life to the next. In the West Eve was condemned by God for freely choosing to disobey his instruction not to eat the apple. Worse still, her punishment was passed down to all of us, and womankind in particular.

St Augustine saw us all as fallen creatures, blighted by a sexually transmitted disease called sin, but not before he had sown his own wild oats. John Calvin twisted the screw further by insisting that saying sorry does not absolve us from our guilt. God had already predestined our fate before we were born, so the only freedom available is to hand our will over completely. This act of surrender gives us perfect freedom, but only by sacrificing personal autonomy altogether.

The politics of freedom

Religion does not on the whole offer much to satisfy Daltrey's cry for freedom but gradually, about four hundred years ago, new voices began to be heard in Europe. After centuries of repression, downtrodden peasants began to insist they were not born with saddles on their backs, nor should any man live in fear. The scent of liberty was in the air, deriving from the Latin *liber*, a free man, not a slave.

Other social changes were happening too. Worshippers began to read the Bible for themselves, merchants to engage in free enterprise, artists to paint portraits of recognisable individuals, poets to express private feelings, diarists to record their intimate thoughts, and claimants to demand their personal dues in court.

These shifts in consciousness helped to revive the Ancient Greek idea of democracy. It excluded women and slaves, but to it we owe our modern rights to speak freely, benefit from our labour, meet with like-minded people, be justly treated and believe what we want. The principle of equal liberty guarantees our access to clean air, fresh water, meaningful work and essential dignity.

George Orwell

1903–50

Orwell's fiction introduced us to Big Brother and the Thought Police, devices used by totalitarian governments not just to crush freedom of thought but to make the very idea of freedom unthinkable. He would be shocked at how we have given Big Brother access to our private lives without a shred of resistance.

These entitlements have not come without a fight, and many have died to win the right to make their voice heard in the ballot box. By choosing not to vote, distracted by the very freedoms and pleasures which democracy grants us, we run the risk of letting in the worst leaders by default. The best way to protect our right to vote is to ask awkward questions, engage with the issues, maintain the fight for a free press and make sure our voice is heard. The best way to lose our vote is to do none of these things.

In one-party states a few risk their lives to speak out, but the vast majority are brainwashed into fearing it as a burden too great to bear. There are no meaningful elections because those who resist are liquidated or neutralised through thought control. George Orwell imagined a dystopian future where the phrase 'freedom of thought' is not an idea that can be expressed, because the words have been removed from the language.

In the democratic West a dynamic alliance has developed between individual liberty, universal rights, free trade, the creation of wealth, the open circulation of ideas and regular elections. This can be a chaotic process, criticised by some for introducing mediocrity and majority mob rule. If left to popular vote for instance, more prisons would be built and the death penalty reinstated. In these situations, do 'the people' always know best? And what if they elect a dangerous leader?

Representative democracy tempers knee-jerk policy making by forming parliaments of elected individuals who vote according to their conscience, not public mood. This forms a protective buffer which gives time for measured legislation, considered policy change and the free expression of difference. Most importantly, it allows the removal of a bad leader without bloodshed.

Around the year 2000, there was confidence that democracy would conquer the world as the fairest and most rational choice of government, but it is still practised by only sixty per cent of nations. The other forty per cent quote electoral turmoil and inability to appoint a strong leader as reasons for avoiding it.

Despite its shortcomings, democracy remains our most freedom-preserving form of government, infinitely preferable to tyranny and anarchy. It is a mutual association of free beings valued as ends in themselves, and the separation of powers prevents any one faction from taking over while also providing a strong unitary authority that has to answer for its actions every four or five years.

Freedom and responsibility

In the eyes of the law, moral freedom is a fundamental principle, not as something we can prove by argument but as a value we must assume if personal responsibility for our actions is to be a meaningful concept. Locking up someone who couldn't have acted otherwise because of a tumour pressing down on their amygdala causing them to behave pathologically is plain cruelty.

Such cases might call for a neurologist on the jury to establish whether, at the time of our wrongdoing, we were *mens rea* or in our right minds. Were we a self-regulating individual in control of our behaviour? Did we knowingly force others to submit to our will? In these circumstances, we cannot lay the blame on our genes, our parents or what we had for dinner the night before.

Political and legal theorists distinguish between negative and positive freedoms. We are not free to drive on the wrong side of the road, but we accept this negative freedom as it protects us from a head on collision with another vehicle. Obeying the laws of the road sets us up to enjoy the positive freedom of travelling to whatever destination we choose and arriving there safely. The same principle applies to drinking and driving. In the interest of the safety of others we positively choose not to have that second drink.

Drinking and driving point to deeper conflicts of freedom between the mind and the body. Our body may be locked in a prison cell but our mind remains our own, and free to roam. Many hostages and prisoners of conscience testify to preserving their inner freedom during captivity by rehearsing their dreams, reciting poetry or writing journals.

Libertarians have a muddled notion of freedom, arguing for minimal state control in public and private life. We can take whatever drugs we like, so long as we harm on-one else in the process. But if we become an addict we end up passing on the cost to those who have to rescue us, which is a curb on their freedom. There are clear distinctions between the illusory freedom of a 'high', the genuine freedom of self-restraint, and the fundamental freedom of living as part of a collective.

Neoliberals are similarly confused. They advocate a free market but usually couple their largesse with repressive attitudes to abortion and sexual orientation, doubling the burden on the poor and minority groups who are already disadvantaged by their trumpeting of devil-take-the-hindmost economic policies.

Their championing of untrammelled exploitation of the earth's natural resources driven by profit alone is also flawed. When we fill the atmosphere with carbon dioxide we pollute the air that everyone has to breathe. Monopolies are great news for the pike but disaster for the minnow. In a tightly-knit society, on an overcrowded planet, every freedom has to be paid for somewhere by somebody else.

Liberals recognise the need for state security, but not at the cost of individual freedom. We might disapprove of loutish behaviour, but that is no justification for imposing an antisocial behaviour order on someone who *might* go on to commit a crime. One day we too might find ourselves arrested without charge with no proof of guilt, and imprisoned for an offence we haven't yet committed.

Freedom and the brain

Despite these wrangles, our political systems, social relations and personal narratives would implode without a workable and generally agreed concept of freedom. In that sense freedom is indivisible, unalienable and irreducible. Without it, we have no grounds for urging children to make better choices, persuading voters to elect wiser leaders or encouraging addicts to reform. We could never trust our partner, express remorse or find it in our heart to forgive, because such acts are meaningless if they are not freely undertaken.

Why then has the very notion of freedom come under fire in recent years, dismissed as an illusion? Neuroscientists point out that, when 'we' make a free choice to lift our arm, our brain has already decided for us. Our conscious awareness of the action comes after the event, leaving us with the worrying thought that we live in the past, and the future is predetermined.

On closer examination this finding isn't as scary as it sounds. If we can't tell what we are going to do next, nor can anyone else, so we're as good as free to do whatever takes our fancy. Also, when we're lost in something that we really enjoy doing, we are so at one with our body that we don't feel we are choosing at all.

The micro-second delay as the stimulus fires across the synapse might be evolution's way of making us feel *as if* we are in charge. It is also our best opportunity to 'just say no'. Before we shoot off that angry email we need a bit of thinking time, during which we might realise that while we are free to vent our spleen, we don't *have* to. If we have taken time to school our emotions, which is tantamount to training our brain, we possess an even greater freedom to be restrained and courteous.

Our brain is a search engine, predicting machine and probability calculator, so flexible response is the key to survival. We don't know whether that object in the sky is a bird, plane or piece of paper blown in the wind until our consciousness, the tiny part of our cortex that is aware of what is going on, pulls things together.

Our conscious mind doesn't need to clock every little chemical exchange at the micro level. Instead it relies on prior experience to give us a kind of knowing without knowing how we know, our actions so in accord with our desires that they feel voluntary. If we deny this existential reality we're heading for determinism and reductionism, according to which we fall in love because atoms blindly form molecules in a neurotransmitter which triggers a neuron which stimulates an axon to send a Valentine's card.

THE STUPENDOUS STORY OF US

Somewhere along this causal chain where upward and downward causation meet, a new phenomenon enters the world, a thinking, desiring, choosing person. From what appear to be chaotic events at the microlevel arises non-random and purposive behaviour. This principle holds true for the whole of nature. Even if we managed to deconstruct all of an earthworm's inner workings, we would still struggle to 'explain' one of its wriggles.

Reductive determinism is a good ploy if we want to find out why our car won't start: it's run out of fuel, which is a pretty good *material* reason. The *human* reasons for our wanting to make a car journey in the first place are much more complex.

Computing and mechanical metaphors can't 'explain' our freedom, because the mind/brain has no circuits, valves, pistons or electric cables, hardwired, softwired, prewired or otherwise. Physics explains a lot of things, but once we find ourselves appealing to random quantum fluctuations or insist that the future of the universe was foreordained at the moment of the Big Bang, we have entered the realm of mysticism.

The only sense in which our actions are determined is our determination to keep them free. Nor are they random, as in chaotic and causeless, because this scenario is just as scary as everything being nailed down and predictable. There *are* causes, but there are also reasons, lying along complex pathways between body and mind, with green and red lights at every junction.

Freedom and the mind

The notion of a mind making decisions on its own unsettles many cognitive scientists, so they opt for compatibilism: there is a body made of atoms, and a mind made of memories. Our mind can't 'push' our body into action, but without our mind's instructions our brain doesn't know which muscles to flex. It doesn't seem likely therefore that our mind is a prisoner of our brain or that our body cuts our mind out of the action.

Brain and mind do not work in opposition but complement each other. We need the biology and psychology working in harmony because our lives don't run neatly along tramlines. Every day we face contradictory, unpredictable, fuzzy and bewildering choices. We are not isolated decision-crunchers but busy social players, acted upon as much as acting, every choice we make influenced by a thousand prior choices.

For all their formulae scientists can't foretell the disordered movement of air molecules inside a balloon, or how particles will behave when they are smashed together inside a collider. There are only probabilities, not certainties. The networks inside our brain, powering the windmills of our mind, are infinitely more complex and indeterminate. We can be sure of a lot of things, but we can't predict what sort of adult a baby will grow into.

Psychologists have taken a different approach to the 'problem' of freedom, and in particular our belief in free will. Freud proposed that our unconscious calls the shots ninety per cent of the time. Social psychologists have shown how our thinking is readily manipulated and often contaminated. We say we are not racially prejudiced, but give ourselves away by our involuntary responses. They remind us that our greatest freedom is to be wrong about ourselves.

Politicians know that we are vulnerable to the 'mere exposure' effect: if we're told something often enough, we start to believe it. This suggests that our conviction that we are independent minds is a delusion, cruel and dangerous by turns. Stanley Milgram and Phillip Zimbardo showed, in controversial experiments, how quickly we can be stripped of our conventional morality under the influence of peer pressure.

Forced to be free

Governments have exploited our suggestibility and gullibility by setting up 'nudge units': how can they encourage us to recycle, eat less meat, use our own shopping bags or swallow fewer pain killers, without making us feel we are being seduced into compliance? We don't like the feeling of being 'played upon', and we know instinctively whether we are acting or being acted on, but we are open to a bit of gentle persuasion if we can see that it is in our best interests. Peer pressure is an effective lever. We're more likely to install solar panels if we see that our neighbours have already done so.

Certain alterations in our mental state, such as intoxication, hypnosis or brainwashing, even sleep, suspend our freedom of will temporarily, but usually our brain resets to default. But *whose* default? Films such as 'The Matrix' suggest that we are living in a computer simulation. The only true freedom is to take the red pill and confront the reality of our delusion, painful as this is. Or we can keep on taking the blue pill, content with the daily round of soaps, takeaways and sporting clashes.

Karl Marx considered that taking the blue pill amounts to false consciousness. We don't taste true freedom until we throw off the chains of illusion and join the revolution. Jean-Paul Sartre's term was bad faith. We get out of bed, put on our clothes unthinkingly as a kind of uniform and present a prepared face to the world because it's easier that way, and it's what others expect of us.

Sartre's thinking was influenced by the stark choices facing his French compatriots under Nazi occupation. Like them we have no essential self to appeal to, only decisions that we must make, which alone determine who we really are. Whether or not our choices felt free and authentic in the past, the future forces us to be free, because it is as yet unwritten.

Determinism cannot come to our rescue, nor can taking a 'morality pill', because out-sourcing our freedom to pharmaceutics is tantamount to choosing not to choose and living as a zombie. True, real, authentic freedom is the only answer, but it has a high psychological cost. Constantly having to choose between good and evil, rooted in our responsibility for the blood of others, generates its own kind of existential anxiety.

Gaming our freedom

Ordinarily we assume a simple nexus between wishing, willing and doing, but as New Year resolutions show it's not as simple as that. Addicts *want* to kick the habit but every attempt reminds them that, though the spirit is willing, the flesh is weak.

When there is a pie in the fridge, we are drawn to it like a magnet. To avoid it ending up in our stomach we must have a will of iron, or not put a pie in the fridge in the first place. Gamblers have to learn to 'game' their freedom as cunningly as the bets they place. If they feel they are becoming addicted, the best way to kill their habit is to go nowhere near the betting shop or racecourse.

Resisting temptation is more easily said than done because free will is not an infinite resource. It's a muscle that gets tired, which is why supermarkets put chocolate at the checkout. We've worked so hard at being good all day. Surely we deserve one little treat?

We see and feel freedom most acutely in our instinct to play, exploring the potential spaces between us and extending the delightful *what-iffery* of childhood into old age if we wish to. Creativity in art and science thrive on imagination, surprise, difference and invention. We could never count all the ways we have of loving each other because our feelings, like our thoughts, are infinitely combinatorial.

Like Shakespeare's character Hotspur, we can 'call the spirits from the vasty deep', but in art, freedom is paradoxically shaped by constraint. Free form jazz takes a tune to strange places, but it cannot stray too far from its underlying structure. Freedom in nature has its limits too. A bird is free to fly, but not to hold a conversation with a dog. We are free to live selfishly, but we don't *have to* follow the dictates of our biology. Love is diminished the moment we make it contingent or conditional.

Freedom grows in proportion to our determination to exercise it, and we set ourselves free to the degree that we extend the scope of our self-mastery. Believing that we are free is a self-fulfilling prophecy, priming us for our next bold leap forward, but where free will is circumscribed or reduced, as in orphanages, prisons and nursing homes, the very will to live can begin to wither away.

Freedom is not therefore a fixture of nature or automatic right, but a fire that needs tending. If we allow freedom to be denied in theory by psychologists in white coats or demagogues who assure us they know best, we must not be surprised to wake up one day to discover that it has disappeared in practice. Freedom's paradox is that we realise its importance only when it is taken away, which is often too late.

Cognitive scientists have given us a new term: neuroplasticity. There is heightened activity in parts of our neocortex when we are confronted with a new idea, or take on a new challenge, in brains of all ages. This assures us that freedom has a long evolutionary history. As far back as our time on the savannah, old dogs were learning new tricks, and passing them on to the young. Freedom has evolved and continues to do so.

13   What can we be sure of?

Sensory perception, scientific method, theory-making, ways of knowing, social reality, reality testing, scepticism, idealism, hyper-reality, common sense.

Is this the real life? Is this just fantasy?   *Freddie Mercury*

> *We become better knowers when we integrate all of our ways of knowing.*

Mixing our mind with the world

'I can see clearly now', sang Johnny Nash in 1971. But can we ever claim to see anything for what it *really* is? Common sense, based on our five wits working together, convinces us that our brain gives us an accurate map of the territory. From our limited human perspective, reality is what we establish through the triangulation of our senses. Seeing is believing.

But when we think harder, we realise that reality cannot be an identical copy of what is 'out there'. There is no little person, icon of a tree or list of words inside our head, nor is there a 'mind's eye' or an 'inner ear'. There are only electrical patterns made from coded signals. Reality therefore is mind-shaped, created 'in here', a construct of our brain. This difficult concept is easier to grasp if we remember that the image cast on our retina is upside down, suggesting that seeing things the 'right way up' is a trick of our brain.

Other animals have a different take on reality from us. Some insects have twice as many colour receptors and bees see purple as yellow. If we were a dog, our world would be dog-shaped. With fifty times more olfactory sensors than us, dogs inhabit a universe of smells. Bats 'see' in the dark by sonar and snakes have heat detectors in the pits of their eyes.

In other words each species has evolved to see reality as suits its lifestyle and survival needs. We see what we expect to see, in which case believing is seeing.

If the world makes sense to us, it is because we project our own picture of reality onto it, which includes our notions of causality, time and space, entities which do not exist in nature.

Take vision for example, a sensory conduit privileged by our brain. Acute sight is not by itself a guarantee of seeing things as they 'really are'. All our brain gets is a play of light off surfaces, from which it must extract sufficient information to make sense of what is out there. A flower's redness is made in our brain, not in the flower itself. In a different light the flower will look darker or lighter, but our brain still sees it as red. When it comes to touch, smell and taste, our brain gives us even more personal 'feels' about the nature of 'reals'.

Perception adds another layer of complexity to how we see. The eye is not a camera but a filter for interpretation, primed by our memories, feelings and expectations. We see through the lens of what we have previously learned, which is why our perception of a thing can double up as our opinion about it, or whether we 'see' the point of it all.

Our perceptions are often imperceptibly absorbed through our culture. Two groups, one American and the other Japanese, were placed in front of a fish tank for several minutes to observe what was going on. When asked what they had 'seen' afterwards, the Americans focused on the behaviour of larger fish in the foreground, while the Japanese commented on goings-on in the background. One group saw individual actors, the other noticed their social context. It was as if each was 'seeing' a different cultural reality. They saw what they had learned to see was there.

When we gaze upon a red rose we see it differently if we have grown it ourselves, arranged it in a vase or emblazoned it on our sports shirt. We might wax lyrical about its scent and beauty, but to our brain it's just so many photons or molecules entering the space of our head. There is no flower inside our skull, only a coded representation of colourless and odourless 'bits'.

This has led some thinkers to worry that we never 'see' reality at all, only a human version of it. We're stranded between an external reality and an internal illusion. But this is to separate the singer from the song, which is both impossible and unnecessary. We make our reality by mixing our mind with the world.

'My love is like a red, red rose' means something to us because we do not live solely inside our head. We are embodied persons who give roses to each other

THE STUPENDOUS STORY OF US

as tokens of our love or gratitude. In doing so, we create an interpersonal reality between us. As well as the real rose in our hand, there is also the symbolic rose of myth and legend. This can seduce us with its beauty, lead us to mystical knowledge, kill us with its poisoned thorn or divide us against each other in a bitter thirty-year war between rival households.

The appliance of science

None of this helps us to grasp the *thisness* of an actual rose. What is it made of? What makes it grow? How does it propagate itself? Fortunately, we have a way of knowing which can assay its physical reality, revealing what a rose really is as opposed to what we imagine it to be. Scientists want to fathom what diseases roses are prone to, what medicinal applications they may have and how they have evolved alongside other flora.

To gain such objective knowledge they need a method, an intellectual tool that combines the best explanation with sufficient reason, based on prediction and probability. It is no less a work of imagination than poetry but it must shine its light on public fact, not private meaning. One is not a contradiction of the other because our mind has evolved not only to interpret experience and nature in different ways, but also to integrate them seamlessly.

The challenge that scientists face is that facts do not speak for themselves, no matter how abundant, and data requires interpretation. This calls for a theory, which means way of seeing, based on agreed principles, without which fact-gathering is aimless. Does the evolution of the rose confirm Darwinian natural selection or challenge it in some way?

A good scientific theory throws light across a wider area than the ground it stands on. It also generates experiments which, if the observations fit the theory, give consistent results, survive being tested to destruction and confirm or deny the hypothesis it is are based on. It takes only one black swan to shatter the belief that all swans are white, and expose our delusion that the future must always resemble the past.

In that sense, all theories are under-determined by the facts, but this is a strength, not a weakness. Darwin knew there were gaps in his theory of evolution but was confident that his successors would plug them. Some modern theories about the origins of the cosmos rest on very slender evidence, but surprising breakthroughs have happened before and will happen in the future.

If scientists are to break into new seas of thought they must be able to change their mind when the facts change. Their models of how things work need to be open to the unpredictability of dynamic systems. Sooner or later someone will come up with a radical new theory which will set science off in a new direction, and change the way we understand our world. When this happens, the old theories are not lost but incorporated into newer, better ones.

Only science has the power to generate strong theories capable of dismantling assumptions which ruled the roost for centuries. Ancient philosophers taught that the stars, being images of the divine mind, moved in perfect circles with no change, but when astronomers started looking closely through their newfangled telescopes they saw a much more complicated picture.

To see afresh in this way they needed three special qualities: an idea of what they were looking for, which relies on thoughtful speculation about what *might be* there; a readiness to experiment, intent on discovering what *actually is* there; and a willingness to overcome their prejudices about what *should be* there.

This last is difficult, because even the most objective scientist cannot escape the fact that all knowledge is personal and all our observations are theory-laden. We can work only within the limits of our human intellect and we cannot avoid bringing prior expectations to every experience.

Even so, after many failures and successes, scientists have put together a 'scientific real' which challenges most of our common sense assumptions. Combining sense, reason and hypothesis, they give us mental pictures of the unseeable which in the case of black holes can be scarier than staring at the face of the Gorgon: time is reversed, information is destroyed and particles are ripped apart.

Mathematicians also live in an invisible world, this time made of numbers, but this doesn't mean they are out of touch with reality. 'Imaginary' numbers help to keep planes in the air and prevent suspension bridges from collapsing. Lines of longitude and latitude are arithmetical figments in a virtual world, existing only on a map, but in the real world they have saved the lives of thousands of sailors.

By combining data and deliberation, scientists and mathematicians are able to go on mental journeys beyond what can be seen, making exciting discoveries about what is yet to be seen. Technology plays an important part in this, extending their senses. They can now 'see' realities that were hiding in plain sight for centuries, such as microbes, nanoparticles and neutrinos.

Quantum reality

Their enhanced vision takes them to some strange places, especially the world of quantum effects. After centuries of insisting that matter is solid, physicists now believe that it comprises empty space in which there are only probabilities, not certainties. Particles are constantly creating and destroying each other. Measuring these events is difficult because stepping into the water disturbs the fish, making us part of what we observe, and reality a reflection of what is inside us.

If this sounds too theoretical, we have to remember that quantum effects are 'real' enough to enable plants to photosynthesise, brains to achieve hyper-connectivity, computers to operate at warp-speed and galaxies to self-create. At the level of the very small and very large uncertainty is the catalyst for complexity and unpredictability. At the medium-sized level where we live outcomes are much more certain, which is why we don't jump out of a plane without a parachute.

Some have leapt onto the bandwagon of quantum uncertainty to argue that reality is what we want it to be, everything is relative and the future is random. This is not how a physicist sees quantum mechanics. It is a weird theory, but an improvement on previous ignorance. It is fiendishly difficult, but easier to comprehend if we don't muddle realities.

The quantum world is the 'ultimate real', the lowest level to which we can strip reality, but in the human world we find that when it rains we get wet, and there's no denying it. Whatever reality is enjoyed by quarks below the radar of our senses, *our* reality is contextual and intimate, not reducible and remote.

Human realities

Our deep connection to everything around us means that the 'scientific real' is not the only real we inhabit. We like to draw sharp lines on the map of reality, so that we can study its parts more precisely, but when we set foot on the actual turf we discover that boundaries overlap, blur and disappear.

This is especially true of social and moral realities, which are not objective things in the world but there by mutual consent, and no less real for that. We're very aware of physical things because they 'bite back': if we kick a rock, it hurts our toe. But we are also aware that people bite back too: if we kick someone, the consequences will be just as palpable.

We might end up on an assault charge, in which case the law will prove it can be as 'real' as the walls of our prison cell. We might have to pay a fine, in which case we will need to rely on the socially constructed reality of money. If our wealth is virtual, we hope our money will be 'really' in our account when we flash our credit card, which is a piece of plastic worth only a few pence.

Reality and facts are often portrayed as counterweights to imagination and fantasy, but this is a misunderstanding of how our mind works. When we are young, fairy tales featuring animals that can talk do us no harm. The stronger our imagination the sooner we arrive at accurate reality-testing.

The imaginary places of storyland or what used to be called *fayrie*, deriving from the idea of the Fates, are as real as the light and sound waves that carry them to our mind. They are enchanted, but they also create a parallel spatio-temporal reality where events are as psychologically convincing and emotionally hard-hitting as in the real world. We totally believe in Winnie the Pooh's passion for honey, and we care about where Toad's obsession with motor cars might take him.

For all ages stories allow us to fall off the ladder of experience time and again without getting hurt. They tutor us in how others think and feel, and enable us to establish mental boundaries. They relate our inside to the outside, fusing the knower with the known.

In this sense, the personal reality we explore through the arts and humanities is as important as any 'certainty' offered by science. In order to grow into healthy reality-testers and savvy knowledge-seekers, our heart needs educating as much as our head. In order to live life to the full we need to be able to move freely between a series of symbolic orders, each with its own way of knowing and being in the world.

The philosopher David Hume distinguished between two types of book: those that deal with 'matters of fact' and those that explore 'relations of ideas'. He mischievously suggested that we should throw the second category into the flames, on the grounds that only science can give us bankable knowledge about why things are as they are. What we see is what we get.

But our inner world is real too. Hume was being provocative because he knew that we turn to the arts, humanities and the great wisdom traditions to explore how we feel, learn how to live together and find some meaning in our being here. Simply 'knowing' isn't enough. Beyond matters of fact, we need the relations of ideas to make sense of our beliefs, joys, hopes and fears.

We also need to stay open to new realities. The wealthy young prince Siddhartha thought he knew 'reality' until he stepped out of his palace one day and saw a sick man, a beggar, an old man and a corpse. In a moment of spiritual awakening he saw new relations of ideas between these old matters of fact. The scales were peeled from his eyes, and he became the person known to us today as the Buddha.

Disputed realities

Sceptics deny us even this kind of epiphany, their radical doubt upending all our supposed certainties. We are the dupes of learned ignorance. Our deepest convictions about what we think we know are fatally holed below the water before we set sail. We may be right but for the wrong reasons. We may think we're wrong when we are in fact right. We may know the answer without realising it.

Benign scepticism can be healthy, saving us from error and arrogance. Individually we know very little and wouldn't survive a week if we got lost in the woods. Socrates taught us to interrogate every assumption that we unquestioningly rely on. He has a point: history has been shaped not by what people thought they knew, but by great unknowns that took them completely by surprise.

Radical scepticism can however be a snake that devours its own tail. Nothing can be known, and even if it could be we have no way of sharing it with other minds. For all we know the world was created last Tuesday. Memories don't disprove this, because they exist only in the present. Other minds don't disprove it, because they might be zombies programmed to play their part in the deception.

Fortunately there are some things that we simply do not need to doubt. If we're making a mercy dash to visit a dying relative we might doubt whether we will arrive in time, but we don't for a moment doubt our wish to go.

A touch of scepticism in the form of honest doubt is good for us, guarding us against gullibility. Convictions are dangerous, urging us to do things we may later regret and blinding us to the possibility that we might be wrong. When we scratch a fanatic, we usually find a splinter of doubt just beneath the skin.

It pays to be capable of what the poet John Keats called negative capability, or the ability to live with uncertainty, not feeling the need to wrap ourselves in fixed beliefs and suffocating dogmas. There is no guarantee that any single belief system can show us ultimate reality, give us a perfect system of knowing or make us eternally happy. Given that we are victims of naive realism, convinced that reality is the sum total of what is presented to our mind and how we respond it, our best advice is to review everything we regard as gospel truth as often as we can.

Total scepticism on the other hand is debilitating, just another form of dangerous conviction leaving even the sceptic with no way of knowing whether scepticism is true. If we find ourselves being sucked into scepticism there are two simple antidotes: pinch ourselves hard and phone a friend.

Freud saw reality from a psychological perspective. We are doomed to eternal unhappiness because we seldom find reality palatable or real enough. We are primed by our unconscious to want more than we can have, but we come up hard against the reality principle. We soon work out that we cannot bend reality to our wishes. We have to 'be realistic', which means cutting a deal with life.

Realist artists and writers try to make this easier for us by showing us life as it 'really' is, warts and all. In 1503 Albrecht Dürer painted a clump of grass with a verisimilitude that had never been achieved before. No-one had ever looked at blades of grass so closely, to see what they *really* look like.

Realism is however no less a perceptual filter than idealism. Idealists are often accused of living in their heads, creating the world as they want it to be, but they are merely reminding us that our ideas shape our reality as much as our material possessions, if not more. Life is very dull when we take everything at face value.

Idealists don't claim that trees disappear when we leave the forest or close our eyes, as if the world is nothing but our idea. They point out that trees are real only as long as we are aware of them, at the time or afterwards in memory. Without our *experience* of them, trees are just so much carbon and chlorophyll.

In philosophy, idealism is often pitted against materialism, but this is a false opposite. It makes no sense to claim on one side that only thoughts are real and on the other that they are hallucinatory electrical signals. Reductionism is dangerous unless we know its limits. It helps when we want to discover what is causing our headache, but not when we say that the human body is worth *just* £10 of assorted chemicals. The 'reality' of a person can't be reduced to biology or what the body is made of.

Some cognitive scientists suggest that reality is a hallucination of our brain generated by our neural operating systems. These are generally fail-safe, giving us a best-fit match for what is out there, but they occasionally malfunction, making us vulnerable to uncorrected or full hallucinations, experiencing things that aren't real, and delusions, believing in things that aren't there. Our brain generally resets to default, like waking from a dream, but in extreme cases such as schizophrenia, loss of contact with reality and hallucinatory voices can be chronically disorientating.

The hyperreal

We are surrounded by images, hoardings, slogans, logos and billboards, not to mention the metaverse of virtual and augmented reality. Will the real reality please step forward?

Postmodern theorists roll yet another hand grenade under our convictions that what we see is what we get. We live in the age of the hyper-real, all style and no substance. Beneath the brands, slogans, logos, neon strips and virtual imagery we are no more real than our latest social media post or computer-game score. There is no infallible view from nowhere, only an inflected glimpse from somewhere. Reality is just a matter of how we adjust the knobs on our receiver.

As it happens we are not that gullible, knowing intuitively that the true opposite of real is not unreal, but fake. When we buy an antique we assume it has provenance and is not a forgery. We're investing in something that is materially old, the more chipped and stained the better. Its value lies in its authenticity, the *idea* that it was made by Thomas Chippendale or belonged to Marilyn Monroe.

Tested realities

How then do we become better knowers and reality testers? There are some straightforward strategies. When we can't agree on the name of a colour we can consult the international colour chart, standardised according to a colour's wavelength, not our idiosyncratic insistence on when blue shades into green.

We can insist on justified true beliefs. We've seen it, checked it out, compared it with what others think, then checked it again. We're not just repeating hearsay, relying on authority or claiming divine revelation.

Some things we like to be absolutely sure of such as when the electricity mains is switched off before we change a fuse. Life has a habit however of throwing us into quandaries where such certainty is denied to us. There is no shame in this. Most of the damage done in human history has been by those who were convinced they were right, in which case it's better to settle for being vaguely right in order to avoid being absolutely wrong. We're more likely to learn something new and important if we keep an open mind.

Mostly we rely on common sense to give us a dependable picture of the world. It tells us that we are stationary and that the moon and the sun are the same size. Science is our only means of challenging these assumptions. We are standing on a revolving globe, and the sun is four hundred times bigger than the moon because it is four hundred times further away.

This does not mean that common sense makes fools of us. It gives us our first taste of things and it works brilliantly in 'common' situations. It is a three legged stool propped up by physical objects, subjective feelings and the confirmation of other minds. The stool falls over only when one of these legs gives way.

We can't afford to fall over so evolution has bequeathed us certain core assumptions which we call tacit knowledge. We don't know how we acquire it, but it comes as part of the package of being a minded body or an embodied mind. We just *know* this stuff.

If we drop something, it will fall to the floor. If we leave our house for an hour, the things inside it won't cease to exist. Up is higher than down. When we turn on the tap, water will run out, not blood or oil. If we see someone in pain, we know they must be hurting. If someone does us a favour, we are morally bound to return it. When we're awake, we know we are not dreaming. What helps us to flourish is likely to work for others, which makes them entitled to it too.

Common sense also gives us a folk wisdom that our grandmother would be proud of: an apple a day *does* help to keep the doctor away. But outside common experience, common sense can be very wrong, sometimes scandalously so. Twelve thousand witches were burned or drowned in the Middle Ages in Europe, some say twice as many, by people who were convinced they 'saw sense'. Common sense in these instances is merely prejudices that haven't yet been 'outed' but badly need to be.

We can't therefore rely totally on common sense or take it as the final backstop of what we can be sure of, which is not to say that it is the deception of an evil demon or the delusion of a halfwit. We need common sense to prove to ourselves that we are not on the set of The Truman Show. And if like Johnny Nash we are going to see clearly now, we also need the insights of uncommon science.

The Mind's Reality Show

Empirical reality	The 'hard' reality of sticks and stones or things that 'bite back', accessible to our senses. It is mind-independent, continuing to exist even when we ignore it.
Rational reality	The 'soft' reality given to us by reason. We cannot see it but we are born knowing that the opposite of up is down. It is mind-dependent: it doesn't exist unless we think the thought.
Common sense reality	A blend of empirical and rational realities. When we mix our mind with the world, we fuse the knower and the known. This is the default reality we return to after a dream.
Scientific reality	Science challenges common sense reality. We say the sun rises and sets, but we are the ones on the move. Science shows us realities in the quantum world that defy our expectations.
Personal reality	Our private reality beyond the reach of science. No-one else thinks our thoughts, knows our joys, feels our pains, suffers our anxieties or shares our dreams.
Social reality	Our interpersonal reality, outside of which our personal reality has no context or meaning. Other minds shape and nurture us by giving us regular reality-checks. We are because they are.
Constructed reality	Our conscious awareness of how things are *presented* to us. It is shaped by human 'constructions' as 'real' as sticks and stones, such as language, culture, family, law, science, religion and the arts.
Ideological reality	Our 'reality-take' on how things *feel* to us. It is not innocent but comes wrapped in a bundle of social and political attitudes about gender, race, class, identity and belief. Politically, we see what we want to see.
Moral reality	Our 'Golden Rule' reality, partly instinctive, partly taught to us, but mostly honed by our social interactions. All societies have the same sanctions against living selfishly and harming others.
Ultimate Reality	Reality (with a capital R) in the fifth dimension, accessible mainly by spirituality or faith, which can be driven as much by reason as 'belief'. Many deny its existence or live contentedly without it.
Fantasy reality	Illusions and virtual realities created by our imagination, but essential for healthy psychological and cognitive growth. They are harmful only when we 'lose touch' with actual reality and can't reset to default.

14 Is there anything beyond?

Religion, animism, evolutionary gremlins, magic, superstition, ritual, faith, belief, spirituality.

My own mind is my own church. *Tom Paine*

> *Spirituality is its own way of being and knowing, with or without belief in God.*

Religion as explanation

The sacred groves are deserted, the names of the gods are only whispers on the wind, and long gone is the notion of a soul finding its way back home after its earthly pilgrimage. What began as awe and idolatry, maturing into the idea of a personal deity and eternal life, is now a dim glow of a once brilliant vision. Fundamentalism, mysticism and occultism are the last gasps of long dead belief systems and for most of us, except for the names of high days and holidays, religion barely registers in our secular lives.

This obituary has been written many times, but it is always premature. No society has evolved without religion, suggesting that it is a normal intuition and healthy act of mind. It is a work of the imagination and intellect combined, as is science, but it also plumbs our emotional and spiritual depths. It is neither our salvation nor our nemesis, but a mirror which reflects who we are and what we seek, so when we attack it we are attacking ourselves.

Those who call religion primitive, satanic or cancerous merely reveal the depth of their ignorance and prejudice. Atheism is a recent phenomenon, no-one professing to be a materialist, rationalist, unbeliever or agnostic in times past, because there were no words to harbour such thoughts. It wasn't a matter of whether there was a God; it was *what kind* of God demanded worship. In similar vein, the idea of the soul was taken as given. The dispute was whether we carry it with us through this life, or have to wait until the next one to be reunited with it.

For our ancestors, mind came first, and matter was seen as a secondary show of a primordial intelligence behind reality. We are portrayed against this divine backdrop as inhabiting a personal universe, our life's purpose being to rediscover the little bit of the godly buried inside us. Our fleeting time on earth hovers between above and below, grace and nature, transcendence and immanence.

Today these dualisms feel awkward and unnecessary, those who choose to be religious in an age of science finding themselves accused of putting superstition before the evidence of the senses. Not so, say those who follow the path of faith. Religion addresses ultimate questions of living, reproducing and dying, for which we crave explanations. This explains why, despite attempts to consign religion to the childhood of our species, it is still very much alive, and spirituality is far from dead. The 'Mind Body and Spirit' shelves of our bookshops continue to bow with the weight of new titles.

Religion and science are often pitted against each other, but they evolved to perform different functions. For all its explanatory power, science cannot tell us why fate is fickle, happiness elusive and purpose hard to discern. Religion and science emanate from different parts of our brain and reflect complementary attitudes to the universe, overlapping but not reducible to each other. Both are as expressive of our humanity as our need to know where our next meal is coming from.

Whether as reality or illusion, religion has been an important part of our evolutionary story. It is an expensive adaptation, demanding personal sacrifice and societal resources, so it must have offered good payback. In less certain times, it played a crucial role in allaying our anxieties, and there was no escaping its influence.

To be born meant to inherit a belief system which bonded the group, codified sex and reproduction, calmed fears about suffering and mortality, and promised continued contact with the ancestors. It stabilised communities, established legitimacy, underpinned moral order, met our need for collective meaning, lightened the burden of pain and tempered the tragic sense of life. In short, religion enabled more genes to flourish than it thwarted.

The origins of religion

Cosmologists give us a new Genesis story, evolutionary biologists offer their own account of the origins of religion and psychologists secularise our spirituality. They paint a picture of primordial anxiety: once upon a time we were all animists, living in a demon-haunted world. The air was full of spirits, the isle was full of noises and awe mingled with terror after every flash of lightning.

Gradually the spirits took on a life of their own, as gods, though they were no more than projections of our imagination. At first they were sprites of field and forest, but gradually they morphed into big-bosomed earth-goddesses, friendly protectors of fertility and harvest sending the life-giving rain. As society became more hierarchical, they mutated into angry sky-gods fighting with thunderous voices over lands, loyalties and destinies.

At around the same time, perhaps much earlier, death entered our world, not just as a physical reality but as a terrifying *awareness* of human finitude. Spirit means breath, raising the question of where the spirit disappears to when the body stops breathing. Mortality made dualists and animists of us all, suspended strangely between two worlds. Some ancient corpses were daubed with red ochre, perhaps signifying blood, preparing them for a new life in the next world.

The sense of a tremendous mystery arising from conflicting realities informed our very categories of thought: dead or alive, sacred or profane, clean or unclean, thing or thought. It still plays a role in our progression from childhood credulity to adult conviction that the truth is 'out there', if we but know where and how to look for it.

This quest to find reasons and work out how things fit together was eventually to mature into scientific method, but only after substantial shifts in consciousness intent on seeking the natural causes of things, not weird emanations. Dogma and authority had to be replaced by reason and experiment.

Religion is criticised by some for consistently substituting superstition for rationality, but this is like getting impatient with a baby for not walking within an hour of being born. It was a long and hard learning curve from magus and alchemist, both ancient titles, to scientist and chemist, roles not established until the nineteenth century. Both practised their art by very different playbooks.

This transition is still far from complete and in many ways scientists are still magicians, able only to *describe* strange forces such as magnetism, gravity and dark energy, even life itself, but not to *explain* them. There are many scientists for whom God is not yet a completely redundant hypothesis.

Religious practice emerged in the dreamtime when magic was relied on to fill in the gaps left by rational explanation, which was most of the time. The rains have not come, *therefore* someone must have offended the spirits of the ancestors. Crop failures were blamed on local witches who were drowned or burned, a barbaric practice that persisted until people began to fear God less, trust reason more and not victimise the 'other' for unexplained evils.

Until this happened the shaman was able to take advantage of the desperate search for causes and reasons by claiming control over nature, contact with the dead and power over the future. Voodoo, juju, obeah and black magic expertly played on primordial terrors and insecurities, their legacy surviving in modern fascination with the occult and paranormal.

Sacrifice of both animals and people was a key element of early religion but in the same way that subtle magic slowly graduated into scientific method, so ritual slowly shifted from external practice to inner meaning. When Abraham stayed his knife over his son Isaac he wasn't making a scientific discovery, but he was initiating a profound shift in moral thinking from a tribal deity of vengeance to a universal God of love. From that moment human life was seen as sacred, a core conviction that has not since been overturned.

The local graven image demanding blood tributes became the Lord of Hosts, capable of seeing into our heart. He did not literally need to be placated or eaten. The kingdom of heaven was now within us, with no need for idolatrous observance.

Scientific method is an achievement of high reason, marking a great cognitive leap forward. But we are also creatures of grand passion, with deep emotional needs. We are still pagans, animists and magicians at heart, clinging to our lucky charms, supporting our team mascots, throwing salt over our shoulder to ward off evil spirits, not daring to tempt fate. We still ask the same questions that an untutored tribesman might ask: not just why do bad things happen, but why do they happen to *me* in particular?

Religion and truth

Science gives us empirical truths about life seen from the outside, timeless and universal, as matters of fact. No matter where in the world we study physics, the course books repeat the same formulae. Religion's sacred texts are not like this. They give us opinions from the inside, 'ringing true' within their cultural frame of reference. The colour of our faith varies according to who our parents are, the teacher we choose and our personal pilgrimage.

It may well be the case that, if pigs were religious, they would worship a god with trotters and a corkscrew tail, but beneath their local porcine beliefs would lie general truths that benefit all swine. This is certainly true of the moral teachings of the world's great religions which not only confirm our core ethical convictions about goodness and justice but also codify and supercharge them.

The truths of science are presented to us in the unchanging language of number, anonymous and ageless, but the truths of religion are allusive and symbolic, written into the human story by named visionaries at specific historical moments. Across several cultures, starting around 600 BCE, dynamic thinkers in different civilisations, such as Buddha, Mahavira, Confucius, Lao Tze, Zoroaster, Pythagoras and Plato, began to expand the moral, intellectual and spiritual horizons of their people, urging a turning away from selfishness, ignorance and violence.

These makers and shakers were not all 'believers' or necessarily 'religious' in outlook, which makes it very difficult to identify universal features of either term. Until fairly recent times the religion we laid claim to was a matter of which belief system we were born into. If our religion was a series of ritual acts, we didn't have to *believe in* any one Way in particular. Merely attending the place of worship, chanting the words and performing the sacraments was enough to regulate our life and mark us out culturally.

As religious traditions diverged, signing up to 'articles of faith' turned out to be much more divisive because to verbalise our beliefs, we have to think about them first. This potentially sets up two conflicts, one between faith and reason, the other between ourselves and those who 'believe in' a rival god or pantheon. If we insist there is only one Truth, we will struggle to engage with those who accept that all gods are avatars, and that many roads can lead to heaven.

Language is a clumsy device for talking about the numinous, or thoughts and experiences that lie too deep for words. The greatest theologians realised that any attempt to describe God in human terms automatically limits 'Him' to earthly attributes, such as 'being' male, 'loving' his children or 'possessing' wisdom. If 'She' is outside of time and space, words cannot capture her essence because they require both to generate meaning. Given that God is literally and utterly 'unpicturable', they preferred to think in paradoxes: 'she' is a dazzling darkness, 'he' is and he is not, 'it' is an endless beginning.

An alternative approach is not to hanker after fixed definitions but to be guided by our inner light, allowing our consciousness to embrace the whole of reality, with or without God. Rigid beliefs and words drive us away from spirituality into theology, which has the potential to disenchant the world faster than a book on the history of beer mats.

Religion in the brain

Doctrinal differences evaporate if we can find a way of 'explaining' religion through an examination of our brain. Neuroscientists struggle to offer a credible material explanation for anything mind-related, but this has not stopped some from trying. Our feeling that there is a Real beyond everyday reality, they claim, is a serendipitous side effect of the explosion in our brain size two hundred thousand years ago, and feeling at one with the universe when we walk through the woods on a spring day is little more than a dopamine buzz.

Others point to a 'God spot' that lights up in our brain when we see a face in the clouds. Cases are on record of sufferers with a lesion in this part of the brain reporting religious visions, which labels the likes of Moses, Isaiah and Jesus as psychiatric cases. The 'supernatural' dreams of shamans and 'sensed presences' of prophets might be the result of epileptic seizures or hallucinogenic trips. Voices in the head owe themselves to a 'hyperactive detection agency' in our brain which mistakes random noises for divine communications.

Before the age of brain scanners, sceptics had already drawn up a long charge sheet against religion. It is wishful thinking, not a glimpse of the divine. It is a disease of the intellect, a mental illness, an opiate for the masses, a comfort blanket, a toxic meme, a grand illusion, bewitchment of language, the enemy of reason, a block to scientific progress. Only religion can fill children's heads with noxious fairy tales or brainwash teenage minds to detonate a suicide vest in a crowded marketplace.

According to this 'religion as contamination' theory, belief in God worms its way into our brain because it parasitises neural mechanisms intended to address pressing questions of survival: are these berries safe to eat, will this predator kill me, will my clan turn against me? In our over-active mind these non-trivial questions become magnified: why do bad things happen, will my wrongs catch up with me, what becomes of me after death?

Religion and morality

As European explorers became more familiar with the indigenous peoples they had helped to colonise, they noticed that tribal societies seemed to cope perfectly well without the catechising of priests and missionaries. 'Natives' often went naked, seemed free of shame and did not engage in endlessly destructive wars of religion.

This rosy view of life as a Noble Savage was only partly true, so for better or worse the Church saw it as its duty to spread the light of Christianity to benighted heathens. Like the merchant venturers who had waded in before them however, their interventions produced both benefits and harms.

Some local tribes were deliberately put to the sword of truth and justice, usually unintentionally accompanied by mass deaths from introduced diseases. On the other side of the ledger, centuries of cannibalism, head-hunting, child sacrifice and burning of widows were slowly brought to an end in some cultures, so as well as drawing attention to the bad done in the name of religion, we must also acknowledge the good achieved through fighting injustice, helping the downtrodden and freeing the mind through the teaching of literacy.

This grand experiment in 'converting' unredeemed humanity still leaves open whether altruism is capable of evolving without any assistance from heavenly lawgivers, or what the Chinese call the 'mandate of heaven'. We can't rerun evolution to see whether natural selection alone could have made us kinder and wiser.

What we can say is that we find altruism hard, and religious traditions have served as major civilising influences in our tortuous progress towards making ourselves more bearable to live with. They have helped to narrow the gap between the kind of people we are and the kind we have the potential to be.

We might feel that, when we do right, we are acting in accord with some deep moral instinct, not obeying what some god commands. But we still have to be *taught* to be good, whether by parents, peers or priests. We are naive to think that we have grown up to be the fine people we are today without sustained input from teachers, the local constabulary and the rich spiritual tradition of our culture.

Given these counter-currents it is too simple to dismiss religion as a deliberate attempt to steal our minds or stop us from thinking. It has civilised and comforted more than it has cowed and corrupted. It has been an important part of our story, played a key role in shaping our notions of justice and urged us to care for the vulnerable and dispossessed.

Some say it has failed miserably. Look at the hatred of the crusades, the destruction of the wars of religion and the cruelty of sectarian infighting. Under the banner of faith religion, which means 'that which binds', has too frequently favoured command and control, not deliverance and freedom.

It has striven to convert the heathen and conquer the infidel, by blood and fire if necessary. When European empire-builders used 'superior' Christianity as a pretext for civilising the unbaptised, even justifying slavery, they behaved like all power-seekers everywhere, often crushing older religious traditions that were just as wise and profound, if not more so.

When we reflect more deeply however, we realise that religious thinking is only one function of the human mind, not *the* determinant of culture and history. Violence and bigotry are human, not divine. More have died at the secular hands of Stalin, Hitler and the Red Guards than at the holy behest of a priest, guru or ayatollah.

Stairway to heaven

It is tempting to dismiss religion as standing in the way of science, but the picture is much more complex. The human brain is a great classifier and pattern-seeker. We don't need to think about the difference between high and low: it is programmed into our brain. Out of this primary act of mind grew the Greek notion of the Logos: arching over the chaos of experience is the rational order of the cosmos, unifying all things physical, human and divine.

This insight was refined by Christian thinkers into the Great Chain of Being, a 'master idea' which dominated Western thought for nearly fifteen hundred years, though it is barely referred to now. This is surprising given that it has been our ladder of ascent from the ancient to the modern world, and the inspiration of our progress.

As we climb the staircase we move up from atoms to Aristotle, because each created thing aspires to become what is above it in the hierarchy. The seed of Darwin's Tree of Life is planted here. Just as the sun rules over the planets, so the lion preys upon the lamb. This 'natural order of things' becomes problematic however when applied to the human sphere. There is nothing in nature that justifies masters ruling over slaves, husbands over wives, the rich over the poor or the strong over the weak.

Also modern science stops before the top rung: there is no God ruling over all. This would be to presume a discontinuity or break in nature, for which there is no evidence. The world can be explained by natural means with no need of the supernatural.

This does not invalidate the idea of a stairway to heaven, as it was not really about the material world at all. It was an escalator for the soul, from purgatory to paradise, undergoing an alchemical transformation from bodily dross to spiritual gold.

Few entertain such thoughts these days, but the Great Chain bequeathed us two important legacies. Firstly, it made clear that there is a covenant between man and nature. Our domination of the planet is a sacred trust, not a charter for ownership, and we are called to be its caretakers, not its exploiters. Secondly, by placing humankind near the top, made in the image of God and endowed with reason, it opened the door to secular humanism, or the full expression of human potential once we have outgrown our need for God.

This fired a passion for ever more elegant explanations. Dedicated monks not only carefully preserved the wisdom of the ancients, they also painstakingly established the core principles of scientific method: the world is intelligible to human minds, and it runs according to natural laws which are accessible to reason. Their deliberations are often dismissed as quibbling over how many angels can dance on a pinhead, but without their groundwork exploring the boundaries of the intellect, the 'God of the gaps' could not have become the God of genes and atoms.

We no longer look to God for explanations and we have replaced authority with reason. Newton's laws do not need a God to keep them going, or the consent of human minds. Darwin's theories take us a step further away from the idea of a God-created and human-centred world: we are part of the animal kingdom, and evolution is its own explanation. Religion has no useful role to play in our scientific enquiries.

That may be true, but the American psychologist William James realised that most believers don't look to religion for explanations of why the kettle boils. Science satisfies our intellect, but it leaves us emotionally hungry. We want answers to why there is suffering in the world. Religion in this sense is not esoteric or mysterious but eminently practical. We choose it for its 'cash value', or its ability to afford us a structure to our life and membership of a community.

Religion and spirituality

Cash value aside, for true believers religion is about faith, which is often pitted against reason. Sceptics dismiss faith as irrational, based on no evidence from a God who is deafeningly silent. Why put our trust in things unseen, or commit ourselves beyond where reason and everyday experience take us?

There is indeed no logical answer to why an all-powerful God should care for us personally, or why we should help others in distress. Some say they believe in these mysteries *because* they are absurd, or they don't begin to understand them *until* they believe.

In that sense, faith is father to the intellect, generating its own facts which lie too deep for proof, relying instead on trust, whose truths are not demonstrable and whose knowledge can never be complete, as we discover when we fall in love. All we have to fall back on is personal experience, which is our principal arbiter between certainty and doubt.

Faith is also deeply emotional, more about living compassionately and making sacrifices for the common good than sheltering behind ritual or spinning intellectual webs. For genuine believers choosing the path of faith is a passionate, demanding and risky gamble. Their faith is neither blind nor irrational, but sighted and reasonable. Nor is it an either/or mechanism. It runs along a continuum, some of its greatest advocates experiencing dark nights of the soul during their long journey to the light.

We are not creatures who believe *anything*, regardless of its credentials. The belief engine that we call our brain constantly tests hypotheses and evaluates different interpretations of reality. This is never a cut-and-dried operation because it sets up a circular feedback. Once we commit to something, it becomes self-affirming. If we believe life is worthwhile we will start to live a worthwhile life, because our belief will make it so. In addition, once we have invested ourselves emotionally we become determined to defend our beliefs at all costs.

Given that there is no compelling evidence for the existence of God, or proof that matter is all there is, we have to resort to trust guided by reason. There is just enough light to cheer believers that something lies beyond their senses, and just enough shadow to convince sceptics that there isn't.

Neither side can come up with a killer argument or knockout blow. Impartial science merely presents us with sets of facts, but how we respond to them, which is a matter of feeling, cannot be put to the scalpel of objective truth. This might explain why many of us exercise a wry wariness as the fairest and most sensible attitude to the claims of religion.

It's worth remembering that the great religions of the world began as outliers, presented to credulous minds as paranormal events, weird prophecies and strange cults. Few of these entered the mainstream, and if they did it was only because they were normalised through the passage of time, number of converts, subtle myth-making and official approval. They also arose at a pivotal time when modern consciousness was taking shape. Anyone claiming a mystical vision these days is likely to end up in a psychiatric ward.

In our own time the philosopher Friedrich Nietzsche famously declared 'God is dead'. What he meant is that the mythical and metaphorical symbolism of words like soul, sin, redemption and heaven, which were never intended as literal descriptions of the world, has been hollowed out by materialist science. We are left with crumbling spires, archaic rituals and sacred art, all very beautiful but drained of their spiritual content.

'Ole time religion' has had to give way to poetic naturalism. Reality is still magical, but in a very different way. The mysterious intentions of an invisible God have been replaced by the visible marvels seen through electron microscopes, in particle colliders and via satellite images of a universe still creating itself.

Glimpsing such wonders still has a 'spiritual' resonance for many, as do those moments when we get lost in our favourite activity, meditate, spend time with loved ones, gaze upon the stars, lose ourselves in dreams or reflect on the riddle of our being here.

Friedrich Nietzsche

1844–1900

Nietzsche boldly announced that 'God is dead'. He was not executing a deity but passing judgment on the way we think and talk about God. Given that God is a projection of our mind and spiritual needs, not a physical entity, He cannot die as such, only be reinvented. In this sense, He evolves alongside and suffers with his creation.

Shakespeare lived on the cusp of the modern world, during the transition from astrology to astronomy, so his plays are peopled by fairies, sprites, demons and ghosts as well as mere mortals. We do not however dismiss his imaginary realm as childishness or foolishness, because no matter how tough-minded we think we are, we still fall under his spell in the theatre.

It's never too late to see a blinding light on the Road to Damascus, not because we've suffered a bang on the head, but because we've kept an open mind. Spirituality survives, not as creeds and dogmas swallowed whole, accessed only through

THE STUPENDOUS STORY OF US

priests, rabbis, imams and gurus, but as a way of seeing into the life of things, reconnecting with ourselves and each other.

Our sense of possessing a soul lives on as a deep connection between our body and mind. We're not just feeling machines or disembodied thoughts passing into the ether. We often experience moments when we feel there is an unexplained presence in our lives, or when reality seems momentarily transformed.

This sense of elevation is a natural feature of the brain, perfectly healthy-minded, and there is no reason not to call it spiritual. We can't explain it rationally but it is real enough for psychologists to describe it as oceanic feeling, participation mystique, state of flow, being in the moment, feeling 'twice born' or enjoying an epiphany. Such 'spots of time' can provide meaning in an otherwise vast and impersonal universe.

Perhaps spirituality is a cognitive faculty given only to a few, like being born with perfect pitch. But we can all improve at finding inner peace and deeper interpersonal connectedness, with no particular sacred text in hand or dogmatic axe to grind. Like the great mystics, we can teach our eyes to alter what they see, perhaps to glimpse a world in a grain of sand.

Retreats, meditation classes, mindfulness training and spiritual exercises can help us to tap into ways of being that not only help us to flourish psychologically but also to live together more compassionately. These are the two deep concerns that gave rise to religion in the first place, neither of which can be broken down to their constituent parts in the pages of a science textbook.

15 How might our story end?

Progress, technology, the environment, the internet, artificial intelligence, the Singularity, trans-humanism.

In my beginning is my end. *T S Eliot*

> *Given our struggle to cope with the problems we already know about, our real concern should be how to prepare for the ones we don't yet know about.*

The lessons of history

We are an optimistic species, powered by the idea of progress. Optimism used to signify the belief that we live in the best of all possible worlds, but it has morphed into a dream of perpetual growth, based on the assumption that we can not only make ourselves happier but also turn ourselves into better people. Our no-places (utopias) have become good places (eutopias).

There are plenty of bad places (dystopias) out there too, nightmares about mind control, the rule of the machine and environmental catastrophe. For the moment however we have some justification for believing in a brighter tomorrow: we are living longer, connecting more widely with each other, controlling the forces of nature and enjoying higher levels of creature comforts. We no longer send children down coal mines or attend public executions. We wait patiently in line and dine with a knife and fork.

It remains a moot question whether this amounts to moral progress. Are we absolutely sure we won't revert to slavery or homophobia? Does our sunny outlook extend beyond privileged liberals who can afford to claim they have banished their prejudices? Our core nature has barely shifted since the characters of Greek drama played out their dark passions at the end of the Bronze Age. We are just as vulnerable to their rages and still guilty of overweening pride, with no obvious ascent from brutality to kindness.

Our misplaced hope stems partly from our belief that evolution underwrites a steady march from simplicity to complexity, with humans in the vanguard. Biologists point to a different truth: evolution has no goals or direction, only an opportunistic drift from one state to the next. It doesn't presume to advance, only to adapt.

There is no Grand Evolutioner who saw us coming at the end of the line. We may be the dominant creature on the planet at the moment, but we have no unique manifest destiny. Meteor strikes, volcanic eruptions, ice ages, terrible droughts, great floods, deadly pandemics and mass extinctions have all happened before and will happen again.

Evolution has made us clever but we have not grown wise. The most successful replicators in the long term have been those organisms that live in balance with their surroundings. Given our pillage of our planet's resources, ability to alter our genome and capacity to become destroyers of the worlds we have created, this sounds a chill warning.

Nor does history intend an upward trajectory except through the gift of hindsight. The past is neither repeatable nor a reliable guide to the future. We face the same challenges as our ancestors, our solutions sometimes creating more problems than they solve. Civilisations have fallen as quickly as they have risen, usually for reasons beyond their control.

Historical memory serves more as a myth to promote a nation's image in the present than an accurate account of its past. Missteps on the road to progress are carefully edited out and achievements are lionised. Given that memories are short but grievances are long, we are more likely to repeat the mistakes of history than to learn from them. We criticise the shortcomings of our grandparents only to forget quickly any lessons they tried to pass on.

In the longer term there are no discernible laws or patterns in the rise and fall of empires to shelter us from our sense of abandonment to chance, necessity and the sheer folly of human ambition. The world is too messy to predict and when change comes it is sudden, violent and unexpected. If we could predict what is coming the future would already be here, and progress would be guaranteed. The reverse is the case. Our short-sightedness guarantees that the unknown always catches us napping.

The progress trap

Some believe that progress springs a trap for us. Our ancestors had no idea as they started to drift from nomadic hunter-gathering to settled agriculture that they were saying hello to long hours toiling in the sun, aching backs, poorer diets, diseases shared with livestock, vulnerability to drought and flood, and disputes about land ownership.

Also, as soon as any kind of surplus was created, a social hierarchy emerged in which the haves were able to lord it over the have-nots. Some see this inequality as the natural way of the world: life was never meant to be fair, and there will always be someone better off than us. Others see it as the moment when, as the philosopher Rousseau put it, we traded in our freedom for the chains that keep us in our place.

And yet there have been many gains. Homo sapiens has never been better fed, so well protected from disease and assured of the blessing of dying peacefully and painlessly. We have almost banished conquest, war, famine and death, known in times past as the Four Horsemen of the Apocalypse which ravaged the lives of the many until quite recent times.

We have widened our moral circle to include those we will never meet. Across the globe nations have signed up to the declaration of basic human rights, though they are by no means universally upheld. More people have access to medicines, clean water and communications technology. Educating girls has been transformational in lowering birth rates, cutting poverty and reducing carbon footprint.

The Age of Aquarius

This is the dawning of the Age of Aquarius, the water bearer. During this age, say astrologers, we will take control of our destiny and achieve cosmic consciousness.

Optimists believe that we have entered the Age of Aquarius when humans will establish flourishing for all through responsible stewardship of the planet and evolve a heightened consciousness that will herald a new age of enlightenment.

Global events since 2000 have dented this positive vision. Once we could identify our enemy but terrorists can now strike anywhere, using any method. Truth is now calculated by the worth of our private data to advertising companies. We know that man-made climate change is real and viruses are capable of holding the world to ransom.

We are locked in culture wars orchestrated by ideologues on the fringes, and nationalism is on the march again. The populist revolution of 2016 on both sides of the Atlantic was illuminated not by an Aquarian vision of sweetness and light but overshadowed by insecurity, anger, fear-mongering and suspicion. Governments overestimated the power of rational argument and underestimated the emotional pull of identity politics. It felt as if the Enlightenment dream of progress had been put on hold for a while and the prophets of doom were in the ascendant.

Although our technical smartness has made us into gods, we still have the emotional wiring of our sapiens forebears. It took a million years to perfect the axe but once it took off as a cultural artefact, whether as a lever to change the world or a weapon to strike our enemies, it outpaced biological adaptation by a factor of ten thousand. Ever since we have been playing psychological and moral catch-up with each new technology as it appears,

Initially seen as a kind of magic, new technology is so powerful that it becomes an unstoppable force for change before we have time to evaluate it, rushed in before there is time to agree protocols, practices and principles. We regard what *can* be done as much more exciting than what *should* be done. The motor car was born of the love of speed but not far behind were driving tests, speed limits, seat belts and highway codes, not to mention urban air pollution, traffic jams, spaghetti junctions and a million deaths on the road every year.

We shouldn't however make technology the villain of the piece. Having helped us to foul our own nest, it may be the saving of us yet. Genetic engineering, despite malign publicity that it will produce rampant superweeds, is capable of creating organisms and plants that can suck carbon out of the atmosphere, cleanse polluted seas, flourish in marginal soils, feed twice as many, and provide alternatives for our dwindling supply of antibiotics.

Neither good nor bad, technology merely exaggerates the virtues and vices that are already within us. It may enrich how we think and interact with each other or persuade us that reduced contact in the flesh is a fair price to pay for living alone in the virtual crowd. The one thing it can't do is exorcise our evolutionary gremlins or make us better people. For every crowd-funding campaign that saves the life of a sick child, there is a scammer stealing the life savings of a vulnerable pensioner.

The Achilles heel of technology is that, like progress, evolution and history, it has no idea where we are heading, only a knack for making us want more of it, generating unintended consequences in the process. Whether it leads us from the front or pushes us from behind, it always takes us to a destination unknown.

Savvy digital citizens

Technology lures us with its promise of omnipotence. We can see further, explore virtual realities, work shorter hours, take a daytrip to the moon and live longer, possibly forever. What's not to like about being more noticed, accessing more information and never having to look something up in a book?

Quite a lot, as it turns out. The internet was originally envisioned as a giant brain that would spread the love, democratise knowledge and connect the whole planet. For many it is the triumph of liberalism and reason.

Our Faustian pact with cyber-utopia has not however worked out like this. Disruption can be creative but when let loose on our jittery attention spans, it can be seriously distracting. Instead of encouraging us to think for ourselves, which is hard, it has proved easier to allow algorithms to do our thinking for us.

We end up in the panopticon, viewed from all sides, acting as our own surveillance officers, lured into caring about things we don't really care about and in need of a digital detox. We disappear deeper into the metaverse, cocooned and marooned, mistaking the colonisation of our mind for the elixir of of immortality. The internet's greatest asset is its freedom, but every freedom has a cost. In this case it is our sense of self discovery and the time that we might have spent with people in the real world.

Perhaps we should have foreseen how a device originally intended to send out a message about the next committee meeting would spew out the malice of deep fakes, chatbots, trolling, sexting, cyber-bullying, internet silos, clickbait, ransomware, revenge porn and the dark web. Maybe we should have anticipated the digital Wild West where truth is a matter of opinion, facts are optional, bad news shouts the loudest, conspiracy theories abound and infinite data blocks the path to wise decision-making.

We might have guessed that, while it's good that politicians don't have a stranglehold on public opinion, it's dangerous when the only opinions that get heard are those that lead because they bleed. We should have intuited that search engines would direct us not to news and views that broaden our understanding but corral us into echo chambers where we all we hear is our own tribal prejudices, sold back to us on the strength of our 'hits'. We could have anticipated that Big Tech companies would follow the lead of Big Tobacco a generation before them, prioritising profit over the wellbeing of their customers.

In the hands of the unscrupulous any technology can be weaponised against us, but we are not powerless against this. We have centuries of moral argument and democratic experience on our side. In the public realm, we do not allow our children to be exposed to harm. Instead we call out hate speech when we hear it, insist on our privacy, expect truth to be upheld and believe in fair competition. The digital and virtual worlds have to be held to the same account, even if it takes a while for our laws to catch up.

If the spreaders of hate and fabricators of falsehood are not to prevail, *we* have to catch up too, as mindful and savvy digital citizens, intent on keeping cyberspace open, collaborative and free of predators. Libertarians insist that anything goes, but as a society we are not laissez faire about drugs, speeding, food additives, slander, constant surveillance or attempts to undermine our freedom.

We care what kind of world our children will grow up in, and the best way of safeguarding this is to resist contamination of our thinking and pollution of the public sphere. This is not to deny freedom of expression or plead for censorship. It is to defend fact-seeking and truth-telling as rational and achievable practices in a pluralist society.

We also need a better model for the stewardship of the world's knowledge, as pioneered by the voluntary editors of Wikipedia. As more and more information is hoarded digitally by a handful of billionaires with more influence and power than any elected authority, we need to know how it is being shared, how it is being curated for future generations, and what protections are in place for when the system goes down.

The Anthropocene

Our concern for our psychological health and democratic freedom is mirrored in our growing awareness that we are not mysteriously detached from nature, but intricately connected to the great web of life. The global commons of oceans, forests, ice caps, seabeds and fresh air are not inexhaustible resources, there to be exploited or polluted, but delicate ecosystems that we hold in trust for those not yet born. Cutting down one tree fuels one family for a year, but axing a whole forest is ecocide, blighting an entire community for a generation.

Our future depends on our understanding that the life support system that we call our home is ailing, and we are the cause of the disease. Gaia or Mother Earth is in many ways self-sustaining, but we have been undermining her resilience since we trampled on her with our first pair of shoes. Now our global footprint lands with ever increasing heaviness on her delicate surface.

Many environmental scientists fear that we have ushered in the Anthropocene, the geological epoch in which all life on earth is suffering the effects of human activity. We are pushing the planet's complex systems to a tipping point beyond which slow change becomes irreversible catastrophe. The sixth Great Extinction looms unless we wake up to the fact that endless growth is not a sustainable model for our fragile planet.

Things are out of balance. We need a new geopolitical consensus based on long-term conservation, not short-term market forces which cannot alone solve our problems. Intervention is needed, but the prospects are not good. Instead of working together to save the planet for posterity, nationalist governments vie with each other for dwindling resources. Our voting systems do not encourage the political structures necessary for thinking globally and the leaders we elect, or who appoint themselves, lack the moral vision to rise to the task.

Some days we might feel convinced that technology can offer us solutions to all our challenges, others we are made acutely aware that it is part of the problem. In what is known as the revenge effect, we feel we have to run faster to stay in the same place. We are better kitted out and safer than ever but also less secure, busy managing our tools when they should be managing things for us. We fear for our jobs, can't fathom how simple things have become so complicated, and fret about the power we are unleashing.

Human machines

Nowhere is this tension more evident than in the field of artificial intelligence, or machine learning. Boffins have long trumpeted that the world can ultimately be stripped down to numbers, algorithms and information. If the universe runs to predictable laws, perhaps aspects of human thinking are similarly reducible and replicable. That prospect is now a reality, with AI's controlling our air space, animating our iphone, guarding our finances and hacking the DNA of viruses.

Doctors readily admit that an AI with access to every case history can make a more accurate diagnosis than an overworked general practitioner. Judges are less likely to admit that an AI can give a fairer verdict than a jury, but it is likely to be more consistent.

The technology already exists to drive cars, trucks, trains and planes with no human being at the controls because such activities are computable. Neural networks made of silicon can emulate human learning, crunching millions of data to infer patterns. All an AI needs to do is recognise an obstacle in the road and stop in time. It doesn't need to have a concept of how a dog walker differs from a dog, or why humans choose to walk dogs in the first place.

Eventually we will learn to trust our safety to a set of algorithms, even agree to be cared for by a robot which can read our every need and mood. As more and more of us live to a lonely old age, with not enough young carers, our only home help and companionship might be a friendly zombie android which never tires or gets depressed, never gets our medication wrong, doesn't give us any lip and automatically knows how to cheer us up.

It is a different debate altogether whether we should ever program consciousness and emotion into a machine, endowing it with beliefs, motives and desires. Some insist that making a conscious machine is within our grasp, just a matter of time and scale, though their claims usually founder on what they mean by 'conscious'.

Others believe that there is something fundamentally non-computable about the human mind. Without a childhood, family and friends, an AI can never achieve personhood, or know what it is like to be human. To be fully intelligent, a machine would need to be programmed to be fallible because learning from our mistakes is the key to being human. It would need to have a body because without emotions we cannot make moral choices.

We need only observe a baby interacting with her carers and exploring her world to realise that human learning is fluid and dynamic, not algorithmic and mechanical. Despite the best efforts of neuroscientists and AI engineers, a computational model of mind leaves us far short of the quixotic mix of personality, language and culture that is a human child. A machine is a system, an expendable arrangement of millions of programmable mini-bots. A human being is a protean mind inhabiting a unique and irreducible social reality.

If we do humanise our machines we may find ourselves facing some difficult dilemmas. If our robot harms us, can we sue it? If we harm it, or sexually abuse it, can it sue us? If we set it up never to harm us, how must it respond when we ask it to help us to die because we are terminally ill? Should it betray our confidence by reporting us to a human authority?

We rely on AI because it is so much faster than us at what we might call 'shallow mind' activities such as linear data-crunching. The human brain needs to do this only occasionally, spending far more time in 'deep mind' activities such as getting along with each other, caring for the needy, expressing ourselves artistically and reading books like this one. This is the paradox of AI: it is quick at things we find difficult and we are slow at things that AI finds easy.

Until recently human intuition served as a last line of defence between us and the machine, but in 2016 a computer program called AlphaGo beat world champion Lee Sedol at Go, an infinitely more complex game than chess. Not only had it memorised millions of previous games, it made a stunning winning move at an unexpected point of the game that observers described not only as deeply intuitive but also as uncannily non-human.

Some insist that gifting humanity to computers, assuming it were technically possible, is morally indefensible. The Singularity is the moment when our machines become not only 'spiritual' but also cleverer than us because they will be much better than us at learning how to learn.

They could be our last invention because we won't be able to stop them. They won't make us suspect anything until they are ready, by which time it will be too late to pull the plug. For all we know, just as millions of us now invent virtual gaming worlds online, we might already be living in a giant computer simulation created by tech-savvy transhuman grandchildren as yet unborn. We're not just pre-machine, we are already post-human.

Mechanical humans

In view of this possibility, the important question is not how similar our machines will be to us but how much we want to become like them. Transhumanists, wishing to bathe in the Fount of Eternal Youth, believe that it's time to transcend our mortal bodies, taking evolution to an entirely new level. We already pop pills, perform transplants and practise gene therapy, so why not turn ourselves into bionic immortals?

If we take this path there will come a point where so many neurons have been replaced by silicon mini-bots in our brain that something new is created in nature, neither one nor the other. We will be able to live beyond two hundred and experience reality in ways our ancestors could barely dream of. We might end up as pure mind with nothing to do all day but sit and think about how intelligent and indestructible we are.

For many this is their idea of hell and a betrayal or our biological heritage. Technology has the potential to be a great leveller, but transhumanism threatens to divide society into a techno-elite who are wealthy enough to turn themselves into deathless chimaeras, and an underclass who either can't afford cyber-immortality or are determined to continue as unreconstructed and flawed human beings.

To date these scenarios provide Hollywood screenwriters with lots of ideas for scary plots: production lines of synthetic human organs for sale, racks of cloned babies, bevies of bionic sex maidens, silos of unstoppable hypersonic missiles, phials of microbial bots that reduce flesh to mush. In real life we may be saved from such Armageddon by that which lies closest to our heart and deepest in our genome: our desire to live *as people* and experience each other *in person*.

Silicon Valley has beguiled us with wearable tech, ebooks, Zoom calls, immersive headsets, augmented reality, even the promise of being 'beamed up' into the artifice of eternity. In the end however we prefer the human touch, not remote cyberspace in which we feel more like a replicant than a person. We like the feel of a book in our hand, the smell of each other, the raised eyebrow that is visible only when we are up close and personal.

We don't applaud our television at the end of a drama as it's just a device, a bit of fancy electronics. We don't mistake the medium for the message. But we do cheer at the end of a live show because we want the performers to know that our minds have connected with theirs.

'Voluntary simplicity', or positively choosing to stay human, might become more difficult as quantum computing begins to dwarf current processing capacities. We won't be able to talk to each other, spend cash or go anywhere unless we're plugged into the machine. Instead of using the Turing test to see if the machine can pass as being intelligent, the machine will examine us to establish whether we are up to the job of being human.

Quantum computing will bring obvious gains of hyper-connectivity and data-security, but some fear a crypto-apocalypse in which terrorists, hackers, criminals, sexual predators and rogue states will be able to operate with impunity, controlling world economies with 'dark money'. Trusting everything to one giant brain also runs the risk that, when something goes wrong, which it almost certainly will, the consequences will be catastrophic.

Immanuel Kant urged us at the start of our scientific adventure to 'dare to know', but he can't have imagined our Stupendous Story might end like this. Mindful of the three questions that Gauguin posed a hundred years after him, he would urge us not to lose sight of our basic humanity as the measure of all things. We ought not to rush ahead but pause to understand where we have been, ponder where we are now and reflect deeply on where we think we are going.

It may be that our future lies in cities spread through the galaxy after our fragile 'pale blue dot' has become spent and uninhabitable, scorched by fire, crushed by ice or blasted by an asteroid. Or we could dig where we stand, investing in making our planet a safe place for our children to play for generations to come.

Epilogue

There is no conclusion as there will always be something new washing in on the next tide, perhaps an occasional piddock-stone or two. These rock sculptures, slightly bigger than a golf ball, lie scattered through the shingle of the beach where I live in the south of England.

Piddocks are small clams which use the cutting edges of their shells to bore their way into pebbles as hard as obsidian, often clean through to the other side. They vindicate Lucretius's view on the Nature of Things and Darwin's theory of Evolution by Natural Selection. While it is unlikely that a Designer God would dream up so fantastic a ploy to escape the jaws of a predator, piddocks have discovered for themselves the benefits of encasing themselves in some of the toughest material on the planet.

Piddock stones

Sometimes referred to as hag stones, these strange rock sculptures are not made by witches but by long slender clams which are trying to avoid becoming someone's lunch.

They have been doing so since the Jurassic Age and will continue long after we are gone. Do they ponder Gauguin's questions about the meaning of it all as they grind their way through the wormholes of Deep Time? How do they entertain themselves in their hidey-holes, celebrate their birthdays or stay in touch with what is going on in the rest of piddock-world?

While I was writing this book I walked the beach every day gathering the occasional piddock-stone. When I had several I strung them into a makeshift necklace, casual but composed, a bit like the chapters of this book. This is what humans have always done, crafting a narrative where none existed before, imposing order on randomness, trying to hold back the tide if only for a brief lifetime.

One day I found a stone that looked like a face, with holes for eyes and mouth, suggesting that even piddocks have ambitions to turn nature into art. But that's another stupendous story altogether.

Suggested Reading

Many have written accessible accounts of the Big Bang or penned dire warnings about Big Brother, too numerous to read in a single lifetime. What we need is an idiot's guide to their main ideas and concerns.

I am qualified to compile such a list because I am a fully paid-up idiot. I could not have written this book without the insights of the authors listed here. Although I mention only one book for each, most have written extensively on their subject and many run websites which direct us towards reliable digital sources.

Andersen, Walter – *Reality Isn't What It Used To Be* 1990 How the electronic revolution has changed our view of reality.

Ardrey, Robert – *The Territorial Imperative* 1966 Stirred the debate about our biological inheritance as a 'killer ape'.

Armstrong, Karen – *A Short History of Myth* 2004 The role of myth in shaping our thoughts and feelings.

Armstrong, John – *In Search of Civilization* 2009 What does it mean to be civilized?

Aslan, Reza – *God: A Human History* 2017 How the idea of God originated and evolved.

Atkins, Peter – *On Being* 2011 A physicist explores science's ability to answer the Big Questions.

Baggini, Julian – *How the World Thinks* 2018 A global history of philosophy.

Baggott, Jim – *A Beginner's Guide to Reality* 2005 Why things are not always what they seem.

Baron-Cohen, Simon – *Zero Degrees of Empathy* 2011 An exploration of the role of empathy in making us well-disposed to each other, and what happens when it is absent.

Barrett, Lisa – *How Emotions Are Made* 2017 The secret life of the brain in stimulating and regulating our emotions.

Bentall, Richard – *Madness Explained* 2003 A survey of the myths that surround mental illness and psychosis.

Berry, Thomas – *The Great Work* 1999 How we must integrate all of our ways of knowing to ensure our survival.

Biddulph, Steve – *Manhood* 1994 How men can express a healthy masculinity without being macho.

Blackburn, Simon – *What Do We Really Know?* 2012 The big questions of philosophy.

Bloom, Paul – *How Pleasure Works* 2010 Why we like the things we do.

Bostrom, Nick – *Superintelligence* 2014 The dangers of AI, and strategies for avoiding The Singularity of our machines becoming cleverer than us.

Bourke, Joanna – *The Story of Pain* 2014 Which works better, prayer or painkillers?

Bowker, John – *Is God a Virus?* 1995 A rebuttal of the idea of religion as a 'dangerous meme'.

Bregman, Rutger – *Humankind* 2019 Dares to suggest that there is a kinder side to us that is yet to be fully expressed.

Bromhall, Clive – *The Eternal Child* 2003 The evolutionary evidence for how we tamed our own violence by maintaining the spirit of play into adulthood.

Bronowski, Jacob – *The Ascent of Man* 1969 Influential television series and book that related science and technology to the human quest.

Brooks, David – *The Social Animal* 2011 The forces that drive our individual behaviour and decision-making.

Brown, Andrew – *The Darwin Wars* 2002 A survey of both sides of the evolution v creationism argument.

Brown, Derren – *Happy* 2017 Why happiness is so hard to define, and why the Ancient Stoics still give the best advice.

Bryson, Bill – *A Short History of Nearly Everything* 2003 An accessible science primer which regrettably leaves out the arts and humanities.

Bullmore, Edward – *The Inflamed Mind* 2018 The links between an overactive immune system, an inflamed brain and depression.

Burke, J and Ornstein, R – *The Axemaker's Gift* 1997 How our technology has both made and unmade us.

Burnett, Dean – *The Idiot Brain* 2016 What our head is really up to.

Buzacki, Gyorgi – *The Brain from Inside Out* 2019 How the brain is not a passive processor of inputs but an active maker of reality.

Bynum, William – *A Little History of Science* 2012 Science told as a story of adventure and discovery.

Cahill, Thomas – *How the Irish Saved Civilization* 1995 Worth reading just to see how such a preposterous claim could possibly be true.

Campbell, Joseph – *The Hero with a Thousand Faces* 1949 Seminal study of how the archetypal hero appears in all cultures. Hollywood directors regularly raid his ideas.

Caputo, John – *Truth* 2013 Why truth is hard to define, difficult to establish and easy to fake.

Carey, John – *What Good Are the Arts?* 2005 Would we notice the difference if the arts disappeared from our lives?

Carroll, Sean – *The Big Picture* 2016 On the origins of life, meaning and the universe.

Carson, Rachel – *Silent Spring* 1962 An early warning of the devastating impact of human activity on nature.

Chakrabarti, Shami – *On Liberty* 2014 A lawyer, political insider and campaigner explains the fragility of the freedoms we enjoy.

Challenger, Melanie – *How to be Animal* 2021 Thoughts on how we need to learn to live with our animal inheritance.

Chater, Nick – *The Mind is Flat* 2018 Why depth of mind is an illusion and our brain makes things up as it goes along.

Chown, Marcus – *What a Wonderful World* 2013 One man's attempt to explain the Big Stuff, based on our scientific understanding.

Christian, Brian – *The Alignment Problem* 2020 How can machines learn human values?
Christian, David – *Origin Story* 2018 Billed as 'a big history of everything'.
Cialdini, Robert – *Influence* 2007 The psychology of what makes us succumb to persuasion.
Cobb, Matthew – *The Idea of the Brain* 2020 A sociocultural history of how and why we have only just begun to understand the most complex machine in the universe.
Cox, Brian – *The Quantum Universe* 2011 Cosmic origins from the perspective of a theoretical physicist.
Cox, Harvey – *The Future of Faith* 2009 The challenges facing Christianity's survival as a living religion.
Crawford, Robert – *What is Religion?* 2001 A survey of claims to the absolute in an age of pluralism.
Crick, Francis – *The Astonishing Hypothesis* 1994 A controversial claim that everything in the mind, including consciousness, is reducible to material causes.
Critchlow, Hannah – *The Science of Fate* 2019 A study of the ways in which our future is already determined by our biology and brain activity.
Csikzentmihalyi, Mihaly – *Flow* 1990 Why having an unpronounceable name doesn't disqualify you from getting in the groove.
D'Ancona, Matthew – *Post-Truth* 2017 How to fight back in the war against truth.
Dartnell, Lewis – *Origins* 2018 How the earth's geography has shaped our evolution as a species.
Dawkins, Richard – *The Selfish Gene* 1975 The book that introduced us to a dangerous meme and obliged us to rethink human nature.
Davies, Paul – *The Goldilocks Enigma* 2006 Why the universe is just right for life.
Davis, Wade – *The Wayfinders* 2009 Why ancient wisdom matters in the modern world.
Dennett, Daniel – *From Bacteria to Bach* 2017 Can everything, including philosophy itself, be explained by Darwinian principles?
Diamond, Jared – *Guns, Germs and Steel* 1997 How and why some societies evolved faster than others.
Doidge, Norman – *The Brain that Changes Itself* 2007 Case studies of the power of the brain to self-renew.
Domingos, Pedro – *The Master Algorithm* 2015 Why AI struggles with what the brain finds easy, and vice versa.
Donald, Merlin – *A Mind So Rare* 2001 How consciousness came to be multilayered in a cultural matrix.
Dunbar, Robin – *The Human Story* 2004 An evolutionary psychologist gives his views.
Dweck, Carol – *Mindset* 2006 Our power to change the way we think.
Du Sautoy, Marcus – *What We Cannot Know* 2016 A mathematician takes us to the edges of knowledge.
Eagleman, David – *The Brain: The Story of You* 2015 How our brain shapes our identity and awareness.
Ehrenreich, Barbara – *Smile or Die* 2010 How positive thinking fooled America and the world.
Elliott, Anthony – *Concepts of the Self* 2001 A historical survey of how the self has been put together and taken apart.

Engelke, Matthew – *How to Think like an Anthropologist* 2017 How anthropology can help us to see ourselves for who we truly are.

Evans, Dylan – *Emotion* 2001 The importance of emotion in shaping our cognitive landscape.

Everett, Daniel – *Don't Sleep, There are Snakes* 2008 An anthropologist who lived with an Amazon tribe for a year gives fascinating insights into what we all share beneath the skin.

Ferguson, Niall – *Civilization* 2011 How, by fair means or foul, Europe manoeuvred its way to world domination.

Fernandez-Armesto, Felipe – *So You Think You're Human?* 2004 An exploration of what it means to be human in light of our animal origins.

Ferry, Luc – *Learning to Live* 2010 Philosophy as a guide to life, not as a dry academic quest.

Foley, Michael – *The Age of Absurdity* 2010 Why modern life makes it hard to be happy.

Foulkes, Lucy – *Losing Our Minds* 2021 What mental illness really is and what it isn't.

Frankl, Viktor – *Man's Search for Meaning* 1946 The testimony of a Holocaust survivor who went on to become an influential therapist.

Frazzetto, Giovanni – *How We Feel* 2013 What neuroscience can and can't tell us about our emotions.

Gamez, David – *What We Can Never Know* 2007 The limits on attaining a single theory about absolutely everything.

Garvey, J, and Stangroom, J – *The Story of Philosophy* 2012 Philosophy as a plot with its own twists and intrigues.

Gazzaniga, Michael – *Human* 2005 The science behind what makes the human brain unique.

Gilbert, Daniel – *Stumbling on Happiness* 2006 Why we look for happiness in the wrong places.

Gladwell, Malcolm – *Blink* 2005 How we often think without thinking.

Godfrey-Smith, Peter – *Other Minds* 2017 A journey into the consciousness of other animals.

Goodall, Jane – *In the Shadow of Man* 1971 Powerful insights into the lives of our closest primate relatives, by someone who spent years observing them in the wild.

Goodwin, M and Eatwell, R – *National Populism* 2018 Why liberal democracy faltered before the forces behind Trump and Brexit.

Gopnik, Alison – *The Philosophical Baby* 1998 How babies are primed to find out about the world, starting as early as in the womb.

Gottshcall, Jonathan – *The Storytelling Animal* 2013 How stories makes us human.

Gould, Stephen Jay – *The Mismeasure of Man* 1991 The limits of science's ability to define and grade our intelligence.

Graeber, D, and Wengrow, D – *The Dawn of Everything* 2021 A radical challenge to what we thought we knew about human origins.

Gray, John – *Straw Dogs* 2002 A swipe at several of the myths we cling to about human superiority.

Grayling, A C – *The Frontiers of Knowledge* 2021 What we now know about Science, History and the Mind.

Greenblatt, Stephen – *The Swerve* 2012 How the world became modern.

Greene, Brain – *The Hidden Reality* 2011 Accounts of deep laws, superstrings and multiverses.

Haidt, Jonathan – *The Righteous Mind* 2013 Why we are so divided on politics and religion.

Harari, Yuval – *Sapiens* 2011 A critical history of our progress as a species.

Harris, Sam – *The End of Faith* 2006 Why faith must eventually lose out against reason.

Hauser, Marc – *Moral Minds* 2006 A probing survey of what gives us our moral sense.

Hawking, Steven – *The Grand Design* 2010 Speculations about cosmic origins and eleven dimensional M theory.

Henrich, Joseph – *The Secret Of Our Success* 2017 How culture has supersized our genes.

Hill, Jonathan – *Faith in the Age of Reason* 2004 How reason almost banished faith, but then underwent its own crisis of confidence.

Hobson, Peter – *The Cradle of Thought* 2002 How a child's mind comes equipped to make sense of experience.

Hoffman, Donald – *The Case Against Reality* 2019 How our brain gives us a 'good enough' take on reality, but not necessarily an accurate one.

Holder, Rodney – *Big Bang Big God* 2013 A scientist who is also a Christian presents the case for God being the simplest explanation for the fine-tuning of the universe.

Holland, Tom – *Dominion* 2019 How Christianity forged the Western imagination.

Holloway, Richard – *A Little History of Religion* 2016 Religion's strengths and weaknesses laid bare by a doubting cleric.

Holt, Jim – *Why Does the World Exist?* 2012 One man's quest for the Big Answer.

Hoyle, Fred – *The Nature of the Universe* 1950 Overtaken by recent research, but still able to inspire and amaze.

Hrdy, Sarah Blaffer – *Mothers and Others* 2009 How the unique primate bond of mother and baby has driven human evolution and culture.

Hustvedt, Siri – *The Shaking Woman* 2010 The novelist and therapist explores the perplexing mind/body relationship from her own experience.

James, Oliver – *Affluenza* 2007 The relationship between wealth, status, happiness and depression.

James, William – *The Varieties of Religious Experience* 1902 Not so much about the nature of God as what we gain from being religious.

Jaynes, Julian – *The Origin of Consciousness in the Breakdown of the Bicameral Mind* 1976 A controversial attempt to explain consciousness which still commands attention.

Johnson, Steven – *How Everything Bad is Good for You* 2005 How modern gizmos and popular culture are not dumbing us down but making us smarter.

Jones, Steve – *Coral* 2007 A polyp's eye view of the intricacy of Earth's delicate ecosystem, and the mess that humans are making of it.

Kahneman, Daniel – *Thinking Fast and Slow* 2012 The unconscious influences on our decision making.

Kaku, Michio – *The Future of the Mind* 2014 The scientific quest to understand, enhance and empower the mind.

Kakutani, Michiko – *The Death of Truth* 2018 The dangers of retreating from reason.

Kasparov, Gary – *Deep Thinking* 2017 A world chess champion gives his views on where machine intelligence ends and human creativity begins.

Kenrick, Douglas – *The Rational Animal* 2013 How evolution made us smarter than we think.

Klein, Daniel – *Every Time I Find the Meaning of Life, They Change It* 2015 As serious as it is humorous.

Kohn, Marek – *As We Know It* 1999 How our ancestors might have seen the world before language evolved and gods arrived.

Kuper, Adam – *The Chosen Primate* 1994 The twin roles of biology and culture in making us who we are.

Langer, Ellen J – *Mindfulness* 1989 A powerful statement of the benefits of mindfulness and meditation.

Layard, Richard – *Happiness* 2005 Why rising standards of living don't automatically result in increased levels of happiness.

Leakey, Richard – *The Making of Mankind* 1981 Putting the pieces of human fossils together in a consistent story.

Le Doux, Joseph – *The Deep History of Ourselves* 2019 An evolutionary perspective on how our mind/brain has taken shape.

Lehrer, Jonah – *Proust was a Neuroscientist* 2007 What the arts have long taught us about the human mind.

Levitin, David – *The Organised Mind* 2008 How to think straight in an age of information overload.

Lewens, Tim – *The Meaning of Science* 2012 How science can and should help us to engage with the great moral issues of our time.

Lieberman, Jeffrey – *Exercised* 2021 Why something we didn't evolve to do is good for us.

Linden, David – *The Accidental Mind* 2008 How love, memory, dreams and God are accidents of evolution.

Lovelock, James – *Gaia* 1979 First introduction to the idea of the Earth as a self-regulating (but now over-heating) mechanism.

Macfarlane, Alan – *Letters to Lily* 2005 A father's attempt to explain to his daughter how the world works.

Malik, Kenan – *The Meaning of Race* 1996 Race, history and culture in western society.

Marcus, Gary – *Kluge* 2008 How our brain is not designed, but the product of haphazard evolution.

Marinoff, Lou – *Plato, not Prozac!* 2000 How the great thinkers of the world give us an alternative to therapy and drugs.

Mcgilchrist, Iain – *The Master and His Emissary* 2009 A challenging but rewarding book about how the two hemispheres of our brain create a unified experience.

McGrath, Alister – *Inventing the Universe* 2015 Why the debate between science and faith still has a long way to run.

Miller, Geoffrey – *The Mating Mind* 2000 How the brain has been selected as a sexual ornament, like the peacock's tail.

Mithen, Steven – *The Prehistory of Mind* 1996 How the mind has evolved as a combination of thinking modules.

Mlodinow, Leonard – *The Upright Thinkers* 2015 Our journey from living in trees to understanding the cosmos.

Moore, Thomas – *Care of the Soul* 1992 Why our happiness and survival depend on balancing the rational with the spiritual.

Morea, Peter – *Personality* 1990 An introduction to the various theories of human personality.

Morris, Desmond – *The Naked Ape* 1967 The book that set the tone for the debate about our animal origins.

Nettle, Daniel – *Personality* 2007 What makes us who we are.

Newberg, Andrew – *How Enlightenment Changes Your Brain* 2016 Neuroscientific evidence of the effects of meditation on the brain.

Norberg, Johan – *Open* 2020 How collaboration and curiosity have shaped our progress as a species.

Nurse, Paul – *What is Life?* 2020 Life presented as 'five of biology's great ideas'.

O'Connell, Mark – *To Be A Machine* 2017 Casting a wry eye over the dreams of cyber-utopians and trans-humanists.

Ovenden, Richard – *Burning the Books* 2020 A university librarian reminds us of the importance of keeping alive the knowledge of the past, and the dangers of losing it.

Pang, Camilla – *Explaining Humans* 2020 Human behaviour seen through the eyes of an autistic scientist.

Pascoe, Bruce – *Dark Emu* 2014 Uses accounts of early settlers to explode the myth that Aborigines were primitive and uncultured when white colonists arrived.

Pearl, Judea – *The Book of Why* 2018 How scientists formulate hypotheses and arrive at conclusions.

Penrose, Roger – *The Road to Reality* 2004 A survey of the laws that govern the universe.

Perry, Grayson – *The Descent of Man* 2016 The artist gives his thoughts on what it means to be a 'real man'.

Pinker, Steven – *The Better Angels of Our Nature* 2011 How, despite appearances, we are becoming less violent as a species.

Plomin, Robert – *Blueprint* 2018 How genes, not culture, make us who we are.

Pollan, Michael – *How To Change Your Mind* 2018 The impact of drugs of all classifications on the brain.

Raine, Adrian – *The Anatomy of Violence* 2013 Do crime and violence have biological roots?

Rayment-Picard, Hugh – *The Myths of Time* 2004 How time means much more to us than the slow ticking of the clock.

Rée, Jonathan – *Witcraft* 2004 How philosophers of all persuasions writing in English have engaged with many of the questions raised in this book.

Rees, Martin – *Just Six Numbers* 1999 How the fine tuning of the universe has given us mind and intelligence.

Ricard, Matthieu – *The Quantum and the Lotus* 2000 A molecular biologist turned Buddhist monk gives his thoughts on how he integrates both of his ways of knowing.

Ridley, Mark – *Nature via Nurture* 2003 Genes, experience and what makes us human.

Rippon, Gina – *The Gendered Brain* 2019 How neuroscience gives no support to the myth of the female brain.

Roberts, Alice – *The Incredible Unlikeliness of Being* 2014 Our journey from a single cell to a complex person.

Robson, David – *The Intelligence Trap* 2019 An examination of the stupid things intelligent people do.

Ropper, Allan – *Reaching Down the Rabbit Hole* 2015 A clinical neurologist takes us on extraordinary journeys into the human brain.

Rosling, Hans – *Factfulness* 2018 How a closer look at the facts can challenge our assumptions about the world.

Rovelli, Carlo – *Reality Is Not What It Seems* 2014 A journey into the strange world of quantum physics.

Ruse, Michael – *Mystery of Mysteries* 1999 The different ways in which Darwinism has been fitted to personal interpretation and ideology.

Russell, Bertrand – *A History of Western Philosophy* 1945 Still a surprisingly readable book which set many on their journey to thinking more deeply about thinking.

Rutherford, Adam – *The Book of Humans* 2018 A brief history of culture, sex, war and the evolution of us.

Ryle, Gilbert – *The Concept of Mind* 1949 A difficult but important book which paved the way for the materialist approach of cognitive neuroscience.

Sacks, Jonathan – *The Great Partnership* 2011 Why science and religion are complements of each other, not opposites.

Sagan, Carl – *Cosmos* 1980 Television series and book which made us think about human civilisation in relation to our place in the universe.

Sandel, Michael – *Justice* 2009 How do we know what is the right thing to do?

Sapolsky, Robert – *Behave* 2017 The biology that makes us who we are, warts and all.

Schoch, Richard – *The Secrets of Happiness* 2006 Three thousand years of searching for the good life.

Seligman, Martin – *The Hope Circuit* 2018 How we are more resilient than we think.

Seth, Anil – *Being You* 2021 How billions of neurons combine to give us our conscious sense of 'this is me'.

Seung, Sebastian – *Connectome* 2012 How the brain's wiring, unique in every case, gives us our individuality and personality.

Shermer, Michael – *The Believing Brain* 2011 How our brain puts beliefs before explanations.

Sigman, Mariano – *The Secret Life of the Mind* 2017 The hidden forces that drive our thinking.

Silberman, Steve – *Neurotribes* 2015 How studying our neurodiversity helps us to be more understanding of those with different brain settings from us.

Singer, Peter – *Ethics in the Real World* 2016 The radical philosopher gives practical examples of how small decisions can make big changes in the world.

Sloman, Steven – *The Knowledge Illusion* 2017 Why we claim to know more than we do.

Smart, Ninian – *The Religious Experience of Mankind* 1969 An insightful and comprehensive account of the world's major religions.

Solms, Mark – *The Hidden Spring* 2021 The neuroscientific quest for the Holy Grail of consciousness.

Stark, Rodney – *The Victory of Reason* 2005 Christianity's role in promoting freedom and enterprise in the West.

Stewart, Ian – *Nature's Numbers* 1995 How mathematics explains the patterns that give us life.

Storr, Will – *The Science of Storytelling* 2019 Why stories make us human.

Stringer, Chris – *The Origin of Our Species* 2011 The lowdown on the increasing proof for the 'Out of Africa' hypothesis.

Sutherland, Stuart – *Irrationality* 1992 Why irrational beliefs and behaviours are universal.

Suzuki, David – *The Sacred Balance* 1997 An urgent plea to see ourselves as part of nature, not as exploiters of it.

Swaab, Dick – *We Are Our Brains* 2014 A materialist account of the brain's role in giving rise to mind.

Syed, Matthew – *Rebel Ideas* 2019 How intelligence is driven by diversity of thinking, not cosy consensus or lone genius.

Taleb, Nassim – *The Black Swan* 2010 How it's the things we can't predict, not the things we already know, that drive evolution and progress.

Tarnas, Richard – *The Passion of the Western Mind* 1991 Understanding the ideas that have shaped our worldview.

Tavris, Carol – *Mistakes Were Made* 2007 How we justify our foolish beliefs, bad deeds and hurtful acts.

Tegmark, Max – *Life 3.0* 2017 Being human in the age of artificial intelligence.

Thaler, Richard – *Nudge* 2008 How we can be nudged towards better decisions without feeling that our civil liberties have been infringed.

Tomlin, Sarah – *What Would Freud Do?* 2017 Different takes on what psychologists and psychotherapists say about us.

Van der Kolk, Bessel – *The Body Keeps the Score* 2014 How the brain, mind and body work as a partnership in healing.

Varoufakis, Yanis – *Talking to My Daughter* 2017 A former finance minister gives his views on whether market forces alone can solve our social problems.

Vince, Gaia – *Transcendence* 2019 How humans evolved through fire, language, beauty and time.

Walker, Matthew – *Why We Sleep* 2017 The science of sleep and dreams.

Walzer, Michael – *On Toleration* 1997 Why tolerance is the way forward in a multicultural society.

Watson, Peter – *Ideas* 2005 A history of thought and invention, from fire to Freud.

Watts, Alan – *The Way of Zen* 1957 The book that popularised Buddhism in the West.

Wax, Ruby – *Sane New World* 2013 A comedian turned neuroscientist and therapist gives her advice on taming our mind and coping with modern life.

Wilber, Ken – *Up From Eden* 1981 A bold attempt to see our evolution in psycho-spiritual terms.

Wilczek, Frank – *The Beautiful Question* 2015 Finding the deep design in nature.

Wilkinson, Richard – *The Spirit Level* 2010 Why equality is better for everyone.

Wills, Christopher – *The Runaway Brain* 1994 The emergence of human uniqueness.

Wilson, David S – *Does Altruism Exist?* 2015 Have we evolved to be kind or selfish?

Wilson, Edward O – *The Meaning of Human Existence* 2014 An entomologist attempts to integrate the sciences and the humanities.

Winston, Robert – *Human Instinct* 2002 How our primeval instincts shape our modern lives.

Wittgenstein, Ludwig – *Tractatus Logico-Philosophicus* 1921 The book that all philosophers quote, and not half as difficult as its title suggests.

Wrangham, Richard – *The Goodness Paradox* 2019 The strange tension between virtue and violence in human evolution.

Zimbardo, Philip – *The Lucifer Effect* 2007 Why good people sometimes do evil things.

Zimmer, Carl – *Evolution* 2013 How Darwin's great idea has faced down challenges and gone from strength to strength.

Picture Credits

p 4   Terracotta Warrior – Jennie Rollings
p 6   Paul Gauguin, *Where do we come from? Who are we? Where are we going?* –
       Wikimedia Commons, Museum of Fine Arts, Boston
p 14 Charles Darwin, photo by Herbert Rose Barraud, 1881 – Wikimedia Commons, The
       Huntington Library
p 20 The Sorcerer, based on Henri Breuil's drawing of a cave painting – Wikimedia
       Commons, Wellcome Images
p 27 Baby – Clker-Free-Vector-Images from Pixabay
p 37 Sir Thomas Browne – Wikimedia Commons
p 47 Polonius – Wikimedia Commons, Typhoo Tea
p 58 Binet – Wikimedia Commons
p 71 John Locke, lithograph after H. Garnier – Wikimedia Commons, Library of
       Congress
p 82 Karl Marx, photo by John Jabez Edwin Mayal – Wikimedia Commons, International
       Institute of Social History
p 92 Viktor Frankl – Wikimedia Commons, Prof. Dr. Franz Vesely
p 102 Statue of Amitabha Buddha, Kamakura, Japan – Wikimedia Commons, Dirk Beyer
p 111 Child asleep – Vectorstock, imagepluss
p 119 George Orwell – Wikimedia Commons
p 135 Hyperreal – Piccadilly Circus – Wikimedia Commons, Steve Daniels
p 148 Friedrich Nietzsche – Wikimedia Commons, Gustav-Adolf Schultze
p 152 Aquarius – Vectorstock, Kasyanov
p 161 Piddock stones – Jennie Rollings

Index